WORKBOOK

Working for over
25 YEARS
WITH
Cambridge Assessment International Education

T0265937

Cambridge
International AS & A Level

Business

Skills

Jane King

HODDER
EDUCATION

Contents

Cambridge International copyright material in this publication is reproduced under licence and remains the intellectual property of Cambridge Assessment International Education.

Although every effort has been made to ensure that website addresses are correct at time of going to press, Hodder Education cannot be held responsible for the content of any website mentioned in this book. It is sometimes possible to find a relocated web page by typing in the address of the home page for a website in the URL window of your browser.

Hachette UK's policy is to use papers that are natural, renewable and recyclable products and made from wood grown in well-managed forests and other controlled sources. The logging and manufacturing processes are expected to conform to the environmental regulations of the country of origin.

Orders: please contact Hachette UK Distribution, Hely Hutchinson Centre, Milton Road, Didcot, Oxfordshire, OX11 7HH. Telephone: +44 (0)1235 827827. Email education@hachette.co.uk Lines are open from 9 a.m. to 5 p.m., Monday to Friday. You can also order through our website: www.hoddereducation.com

ISBN: 978 1 3983 0815 2

© Jane King 2021

First published in 2021 by
Hodder Education,
An Hachette UK Company
Carmelite House
50 Victoria Embankment
London EC4Y 0DZ

www.hoddereducation.co.uk

Impression number   10 9 8 7 6 5 4 3 2 1
Year   2024 2023 2022 2021 2020

All rights reserved. Apart from any use permitted under UK copyright law, no part of this publication may be reproduced or transmitted in any form or by any means, electronic or mechanical, including photocopying and recording, or held within any information storage and retrieval system, without permission in writing from the publisher or under licence from the Copyright Licensing Agency Limited. Further details of such licences (for reprographic reproduction) may be obtained from the Copyright Licensing Agency Limited, www.cla.co.uk

Cover photo © tampatra - stock.adobe.com

Typeset in Integra Software Services Pvt. Ltd., Pondicherry, India.

Printed in Slovenia.

A catalogue record for this title is available from the British Library.

Introduction

Welcome to our Cambridge International AS & A Level Business Workbook. The aim of this workbook is to provide you with further opportunities to practise the skills you have acquired using the AS & A Level Business textbook. It is designed to complement the second edition of the textbook and to provide additional exercises to help you consolidate your learning. It supports the Cambridge International AS & A Level Business syllabus (9609) for examination from 2023.

The sections in this workbook reflect the topics in the syllabus and the chapters in the textbook. There is no set approach to using this workbook. You may wish to use it to supplement your understanding of the different AS and A Level topics as you work through the course and the textbook. You may also use it as you prepare for your examinations. The workbook is designed to be flexible enough for you to use it in the way that best suits your learning needs. You should refer back to the textbook if you need help completing any of the questions as well as discussing it with your teacher.

Many of the questions need more space than is available for your written answers in this book. You are therefore encouraged to fill in the sections with key points and ideas, then write your extended answers on a separate sheet.

A note on the exam-style questions

Exam-style questions and sample answers have been written by the authors. In examinations, the way marks are awarded may be different. References to assessment and/or assessment preparation are the publisher's interpretation of the syllabus requirements and may not fully reflect the approach of Cambridge Assessment International Education. Cambridge International recommends that teachers consider using a range of teaching and learning resources in preparing learners for assessment, based on their own professional judgement of their students' needs.

Skills referred to and used throughout the workbook

This book contains a variety of different styles of questions and activities including:
- practice questions (multiple choice, true/false)
- exam-style questions (short answer, case studies)
- group work
- research tasks.

These will allow you to develop the following skills:

Knowledge

In this resource you practice how to demonstrate knowledge and understanding of business concepts, terms and theories. This may be demonstrated by giving a definition, explanation and also relevant examples.

Application

In this resource you practise how to apply knowledge and understanding of business concepts, terms and theories to problems and issues in a variety of familiar and unfamiliar business situations and contexts. This may be demonstrated by linking knowledge with the circumstances and issues for a particular business in a case study or more generically to a type of business; for example, a family business.

Analysis

In this resource you practise how to analyse business problems, issues and situations by:
>> using appropriate methods and techniques to make sense of qualitative and quantitative business information
>> searching for causes, impact and consequences
>> distinguishing between factual evidence and opinion or value judgement
>> drawing valid inferences and making valid generalisations.

This may be demonstrated by a chain of reasoning, linking a particular circumstance or issue with first and subsequent impacts on a business or stakeholders. Building a chain of reasoning with three or more stages, in the context of the business, will show developed analysis.

Evaluation

In this resource you practise how to evaluate evidence in order to make reasoned judgements by:
- » presenting substantiated conclusions
- » considering short- and long-term impacts
- » suggesting what the final decision may depend on, such as the attitude of management to risk
- » making recommendations for action and implementation
- » judging what may be the most important factor
- » suggesting other information that would be useful
- » making evaluative statements throughout longer answer questions, such as limitation of data or theories, as well as by a supported final conclusion.

To develop your evaluation include evaluation throughout and in the final conclusion, in the context of the business.

To produce a strong answer for a longer evaluative question you should think about how you can:
- – Show more wide-ranging knowledge of the syllabus as it applies to the relevant case study. Be guided by the terminology used in the question and in the case study. Integrate these concepts into the answer.
- – Make effective and focused use of the case study material and/or own relevant calculations, to show strong application to the specific situation/circumstances given in the case study.
- – Provide developed analysis of several points/actions/techniques/consequences (as appropriate to the question and case study).
- – Produce extensive evaluation of all points made in the analysis section, considering both sides, views, benefits, limitations etc. Consider alternative approaches and different actions in different circumstances.

> ## KEY TERMS
> All sections start with either a list of key terms, or a table to fill in with formulae that you need to learn and understand. Do make sure you review all of these before working on the questions that follow.

Answers

Answers to all questions included in this workbook can be found online at **hoddereducation.com/cambridgeextras**.

1 Business and its environment

▶ 1.1 Enterprise

KEY TERMS

Enterprise, business and economic activity, risk, factors of production, adding value, opportunity cost, entrepreneur, intrapreneur, business plan, business failure, local/national/international/multinational businesses.

▶ Multiple choice questions

*Circle the **one** correct answer.*

1 Which of the following is **not** one of the factors of production?
   A Labour
   B Finance
   C Enterprise
   D Capital

2 A fast-food pizza company makes and sells 250 pizzas per week. The selling price is $12 per unit. Ingredients cost $1.50 per pizza and the weekly cost of wages is $1000. What is the added value on one pizza?
   A $12.00   C $8.00
   B $6.50   D $10.50

3 You bought a computer for $500 one year ago. You installed software and games at a total cost of $120. You could now sell the computer for $240. What is your opportunity cost for keeping the computer?
   A $500   C $260
   B $620   D $240

4 An advertising agency encourages intrapreneurship among its employees. The team of developers put together social media campaign ideas and try to sell them to new business customers. Who takes the business risk?
   A The advertising agency
   B The developers
   C The risk is shared.
   D There is no risk involved.

5 Which of the following would **not** usually be included in a business plan?
   A Cash-flow forecast
   B Marketing plan
   C Statement of tax paid
   D Executive summary

Exam-style questions: Short answer

1 Define the term 'dynamic business environment'. [2]

....

....

2 Explain **one** barrier to entrepreneurship for a young person wishing to set up a home cleaning business. [3]

....

....

....

3 Explain **one** difference between an entrepreneur and an intrapreneur. [3]

....

....

....

4 Analyse **two** reasons why an independent tourist hotel business in your country might fail. [8]

....

....

....

....

....

....

5 Using a business example from your country, explain **one** contribution that enterprise makes to the country's development. [3]

....

....

....

6 Investigate a local or international entrepreneur. Explain **four** qualities that made this person successful. [8]

....

....

....

....

....

Group work

● ●

Do this work on a separate sheet.

a Discuss ideas for a new fast-food business, to be set up in your local town. Create and present a simple business plan to the class, including all the key elements on page 13 of the textbook.

b Evaluate the benefits and limitations of your business plan. Will it guarantee business success? [12]

▶ 1.2 Business structure

KEY TERMS

Economic sectors, legal structure, primary/secondary/tertiary/quaternary sectors, private and public sectors, sole trader, partnership, private limited company (ltd), public limited company (plc), unlimited and limited liability, shareholder, dividend, franchise, franchisor, franchisee, co-operative, joint venture, social enterprise.

▶ Multiple choice questions

*Circle the **one** correct answer.*

1 Which of the following would be a business in the secondary sector?
   A A farm
   B An oil refinery
   C A school
   D A fast-food takeaway

2 Which of the following is most likely to be a public sector business?
   A A housebuilding company
   B A food-processing company
   C A railway company
   D A mobile phone company

3 Which of the following is **not** an advantage to a sole trader of becoming a partnership?
   A Shared workload
   B A greater range of skills
   C More capital available
   D Conflicting ideas

4 Which of the following is a key short-term objective of shareholders in a public limited company (plc)?
   A Increasing dividends
   B Increasing spending on advertising
   C Increasing market share
   D Increasing staff training

5 Which of the following is **not** an element of the concept of 'triple bottom line'?
   A Profit
   B Promotion
   C People
   D Planet

Now try this

It is often assumed that purchasing a franchise agreement within a well-known multinational brand is the key to 'instant business success'. However, this is not always the case. Research the prices and conditions for buying a franchise in a multinational brand fast-food company in your country, and create a presentation that answers the following questions about that company:
» What are the roles and responsibilities of franchisees and franchisors?
» What are the advantages and disadvantages of the agreement to franchisees and franchisors?
» To what extent is a new franchisee more likely to succeed than if they had started an independent business?

Exam-style questions: Short answer

1 Define what is meant by the 'legal structure' of a business. [2]

....

....

2 Explain **one** difference between a private limited company and a public limited company. [3]

....

....

....

3 Analyse **two** reasons why a partnership business may want to become a private limited company. [8]

....

....

....

....

....

....

▶ 1.3 Size of business

KEY TERMS

Measures of business size, small/medium/large businesses, family business, niche market, business growth, internal (organic) growth, external growth, merger, takeover, horizontal/vertical/conglomerate diversification, strategic alliance.

▶ Multiple choice questions

*Circle the **one** correct answer.*

1 Which of the following would be the best way to measure the size of a public sector service organisation?
 A Total annual revenue
 B Total value of assets
 C Total number of employees
 D Total annual profit

2 Which of the following is a disadvantage of being a small business?
 A Difficult to set up
 B Difficult to raise finance
 C Lack of flexibility
 D Low motivation of owner

3 Which of the following is an advantage of being a family business?
 A Shared values
 B Wide range of expertise
 C More capital available
 D Easy access to finance

4 Which of the following is an example of forward vertical integration?
 A A food-processing company taking over a food retailer
 B A travel agency taking over an airline
 C A private school merging with another private school
 D A soft drinks manufacturer taking over a bus company

5 Which of the following is an example of internal (organic) growth?
 A A car manufacturer taking over a competitor
 B A farm merging with a food retailer
 C A railway company being privatised
 D A fast-food company opening a new branch

Now try this

You may think that all businesses have growth as a major objective, but there are many more small businesses than large ones in most countries worldwide. Work in a small group, and each arrange to interview a small business in order to answer the following questions:

» What are the main objectives of small-business owners?
» What are the advantages and disadvantages of staying small, rather than trying to grow your business?
» To what extent do small-business owners consider growth as a long-term aim?

Exam-style questions: Short answer

1   Define the term 'business growth'.   [2]

    ....

    ....

2   Explain **one** disadvantage to a business of internal rather than external growth.   [3]

    ....

    ....

    ....

3   Analyse **two** reasons why a car manufacturer may take over a company that produces car tyres.   [8]

    ....

    ....

    ....

    ....

    ....

    ....

4   Shabnam runs a grocery store, which meets the needs of the population of a village in Country X. Analyse one point for each of the following:

    a) The role that this store plays in the overall structure of the retail food industry in Country X.   [4]

        ....

        ....

        ....

    b) The importance of Shabnam's store to the economy of Country X.   [4]

        ....

        ....

        ....

5 Analyse **two** reasons why a housebuilding company might enter a joint venture with a local company when expanding to another country. [8]

....

....

....

....

....

....

6 Evaluate the view that a takeover or merger with another organisation will always bring benefits to customers and the merged company. [12]

....

....

....

....

....

....

....

....

▶ **1.4** Business objectives

KEY TERMS

Business objectives, SMART target, ethics, profit maximisation, survival, diversification, service provision, social and ethical objectives, triple bottom line, corporate social responsibility (CSR), mission statement, strategy, tactics, targets, budgets.

▶ **Multiple choice questions**

*Circle the **one** correct answer.*

1 What does the 'M' in 'SMART' objectives stand for?
   A Monitored
   B Measurable
   C Meaningful
   D Manageable

2 Which of the following may be an objective for both private and public sector organisations?
   A Maximising profits
   B Increasing market share
   C Providing an excellent customer service
   D Maximising dividends to shareholders

3 Which of the following would be a suitable objective for a business trying to recover from enforced closure during a global virus pandemic?
  A Increasing market share
  B Survival
  C Profit maximisation
  D Increasing productivity

4 Which of the following would be an ethical objective for a fashion clothing manufacturer?
  A Provide best value for customers
  B Source lowest cost raw materials
  C Deliver clothing to retailers on time
  D Pay fair wages to workers

5 What is a strategy?
  A A short-term action to improve performance
  B A long-term plan to achieve business objectives
  C A statement of business purpose
  D A realistic target

Exam-style questions: Short answer

1 Explain **one** example of a SMART objective for a new, small bakery business. [3]

....

....

....

2 Explain **one** social and **one** environmental objective for a farming business. [6]

....

....

....

....

3 Analyse **two** advantages to an airline business of setting clear corporate objectives. [8]

....

....

....

....

....

....

4 Analyse **two** features of a social enterprise business which differentiates it from a profit-making enterprise.

[8]

....

....

....

....

....

....

5 Evaluate the importance of corporate social responsibility as a business objective for a social media organisation.

[12]

....

....

....

....

....

....

....

....

....

Case study

•••

Read the case study and answer the questions on a separate sheet.

Mo runs a small chain of street-food cafés in Malaysia. He started with one café that was very successful due to his innovative menu and the excellent value for money he offered. Mo has used the profit he made on the first café to open four more over the last three years. However, in recent months, the government has ordered all restaurants and cafés to close in order to prevent the spread of a serious viral infection. Mo's cafés have been delivering food to people's homes, but revenue is down by 60 per cent. Mo called all his café managers to a meeting, saying 'if this situation continues, we may not be able to continue trading'. He asked the managers for ideas for a strategy to build up the business when cafés are allowed to open again.

1 Define 'growth' as a business objective. [2]

2 State **two** factors that have helped Mo increase the size of his business. [2]

3 Explain **two** advantages to Mo of communicating his business objectives to managers and employees in his street food cafés. [6]

4 Analyse how Mo's objectives have changed since he started his business with one café. [8]

5 Evaluate the best strategy for Mo's business when it re-opens. Justify your recommendation. [12]

▶ 1.5 Stakeholders in a business

> **KEY TERMS**
> Stakeholders, internal and external stakeholders, accountability, social responsibility, stakeholder conflict.

▶ Multiple choice questions

*Circle the **one** correct answer.*

1 Which of the following would **not** be an internal stakeholder group in a manufacturing company?
   A Business owners
   B Business customers
   C Business managers
   D Business salespeople

2 Which of the following is an objective of the government as a stakeholder in a fast-food business?
   A Collecting the correct amount of business tax
   B Helping the business maximise profits
   C Encouraging export of products
   D Helping the business to recruit workers

3 Which of the following is a possible stakeholder interest of the local community in the area close to a supermarket business?
   A Good choice of products
   B Low pollution levels
   C Low prices
   D Good customer service

4 Which of the following is **not** a stakeholder aim for employees?
   A Good working conditions
   B Secure jobs
   C Fair pay
   D Low prices

5 Which of the following is the main priority for businesses, according to the shareholder concept?
   A Increasing market share
   B Providing good service
   C Paying fair wages
   D Maximising dividends

Exam-style questions: Short answer

1 Define a 'shareholder' in a business.   [2]

   ....

   ....

2 Explain **one** right and **one** responsibility of component suppliers to a large car manufacturer.   [6]

   ....

   ....

   ....

   ....

3 Analyse **two** reasons why the management of a public sector organisation might take the views of employees into account in its decision-making.   [8]

   ....

   ....

....

....

....

....

4 Explain, using **two** examples, the difference between strategy and tactics for a fast-food franchise business. [6]

....

....

....

....

5 Explain, using **two** examples, how conflict may arise between stakeholder groups in a clothing manufacturing business whose suppliers are based in a developing country. [6]

....

....

....

....

6 Evaluate the extent to which a theme park business might meet the aims of all its stakeholder groups. [12]

....

....

....

....

....

Now try this

• •

Copy the table below onto a large sheet of paper and add four extra rows.

In groups of three or four, consider your school or college as a business organisation. Identify **five** stakeholder groups and discuss their aims, rights and responsibilities. Now consider which stakeholder groups' aims might conflict, in the short- and long-term operation of the organisation.

Table 1.1 Stakeholder analysis

Stakeholder groups	Aims	Rights	Responsibilities	Possible conflicts with other stakeholder groups

Human resource management

▶ **2.1** Human resource management

KEY TERMS

Human resource management (HRM), workforce plan, labour turnover, recruitment and selection, employment contract, dismissal, redundancy, employee welfare, training, development, multi-skilling, trade union, collective bargaining, work-life balance.

▶ **Multiple choice questions**

*Circle the **one** correct answer.*

1 Which of the following is **not** a responsibility of the HRM department?
  A Motivating employees
  B Writing a business plan
  C Assessing training needs
  D Filling a job vacancy

2 What is a workforce plan?
  A A new project outline
  B A business objective
  C The list of jobs to be carried out by an employee
  D The number of employees and skills required by the business

3 A business has 150 employees. Of these, an average of 30 employees leave every year. What is the rate of labour turnover?
  A 30   **C** 120
  B 80%   **D** 20%

4 Which of the following would **not** be included in a job description for a delivery driver?
  A Must hold clean driving licence
  B Shifts of 8 hours each day
  C Company van provided
  D Based at Dartford office

5 Which of the following would be a cause of redundancy?
  A The employee is unable to carry out their role due to illness.
  B The employee breaks the terms of their contract.
  C The employee takes up a new job role.
  D The employee is no longer needed due to automation.

Exam-style questions: Short answer

1 Give an example of a SMART objective for the human resources manager. [3]

....

....

2 Explain **one** reason why the HRM department of a large retail business may be concerned about employees' work-life balance. [3]

....

....

....

3 Explain **two** factors which might increase labour turnover in a manufacturing business. [6]

....

....

....

....

4 Analyse **two** recruitment methods that would be suitable for a chef in a new fast-food restaurant in a city in your country. [8]

....

....

....

....

....

....

5 Explain **two** advantages for a company that produces cars of training and multi-skilling their staff. [6]

....

....

....

....

6 Analyse **two** advantages of trade union membership to employees in a large public sector organisation, such as a hospital. [8]

....

....

....

....

....

7 Many branded clothing businesses worldwide have been criticised for their lack of attention to working conditions in the companies that supply ready-made garments.

Evaluate the view that profit is always the most important aim of all types of businesses. [12]

....

....

....

....

....

....

....

....

Case study

• •

Read the case study and answer the questions on a separate sheet.

Rohan runs a private international school in Mumbai, India. His school is very successful and student numbers are increasing. Rohan would like to add more subjects to the curriculum, so he must recruit teachers for these. He also wants to recruit a deputy principal to help him with school administration and finance. Rohan wants to ensure equality in his recruitment processes.

1 Define 'selection' as part of the recruitment process. [2]

2 Explain **one** method of selection that Rohan could use to choose a new teacher of Business from a shortlist of five interviewees. [3]

3 Analyse **two** reasons why Rohan must produce a job description and person specification for the deputy principal role. [8]

4 Evaluate the importance of equality in the recruitment process for new school employees. [12]

▶ **2.2** Motivation

KEY TERMS

Motivation, labour productivity, absenteeism, human needs, division of labour, schools of thought, teamworking, hierarchy of needs, hygiene factors, motivators, financial and non-financial motivators, performance-related pay, piece-rate, fringe benefits, job redesign/enrichment/enlargement/rotation, empowerment, employee participation.

▶ Multiple choice questions

*Circle the **one** correct answer.*

1 Which of the following may be a benefit of having well-motivated employees to a business?

   A High absenteeism

   B High wage rates

   C High labour productivity

   D High labour turnover

2 What might help a business to satisfy the self-esteem needs of its employees?

   A Paying fair wages

   B Allowing regular breaks

   C Providing job security

   D Offering job promotion opportunities

3 Which of the following may **not** be favoured by employers who believe in Taylorism as a way of motivating employees?

   A Paying piece-rate

   B Close supervision of workers

   C Division of labour

   D Offering workers fringe benefits

4 Which of the following may be favoured by employers who believe in Mayo's Hawthorne effect?

   A Providing social facilities at work

   B Improving working conditions

   C Paying above average wages

   D Offering workers training

5 Which of the following is **not** included in Maslow's hierarchy of needs?

   A Esteem needs

   B Finance needs

   C Physiological needs

   D Social needs

Now try this

Copy the table on the next page onto a large sheet of paper.

Consider the theories of Maslow, Herzberg, McClelland and Vroom. Each statement in Column 1 relates to the theories of one or more of these four men.

In Column 2, write the name of the theorist who most closely matches the statement, plus a brief explanation of their theory. In some cases, there may be more than one relevant theorist.

In Column 3, give an example of how employers could use an understanding of this theory to improve employee motivation.

Table 2.1

Statement	Theorist(s) and explanation	Example of action by employers to improve motivation
An online retail business is unable to provide safety clothing for workers in a big warehouse.		
A fast-food business has high labour turnover, due to a lack of promotion opportunities.		
A supermarket business has high absenteeism, due to employees finding work 'boring'.		
A company would like to recruit creative, high-achieving graduate employees.		
A new senior employee has a need for achievement (n-Ach) in their first year with a company.		
A travel company has opened a new branch in a town where there is a lot of competition. The new team of employees are hoping to achieve success by the end of the first year of trading.		

Exam-style questions: Short answer

1   What is meant by Taylor's 'economic man' or 'economic animals'?   [2]

....

....

2   Explain **one** advantage and **one** disadvantage to a business of introducing piece-rate in a mobile phone manufacturing business.   [6]

....

....

....

....

3   Analyse **two** disadvantages to a computer games design business of using employee training as a way of motivating employees.   [8]

....

....

....

....

....

....

4 Explain, using **two** examples, how a public sector hospital may encourage employee participation. [6]

....

....

....

....

5 Evaluate the importance of ensuring high employee motivation in a theme park business. [12]

....

....

....

....

....

....

....

....

Now try this

You are going to investigate individuals and what motivates them at work. Is it more about the job, the wage or salary, or other factors?

Work in a group of three or four students. Each group member should identify five individuals (adults) who do different jobs to interview about their motivation at work. Decide on five or six interview questions as a group, and then all of you ask these same questions to your interviewees. Copy and complete the table below for each interviewee to help you record your responses.

Table 2.2

Interviewee name:		Approximate age:	Job:
Question 1			
Question 2			
Question 3			
Question 4			
Question 5			

Once you have finished, analyse your findings and present them to the class.

▶ 2.3 Management

KEY TERMS

Management and leadership, autocratic, democratic, authority, functions of management, roles of management, styles of management, delegation, business culture, laissez-faire.

▶ Multiple choice questions

*Circle the **one** correct answer.*

1 Establishing targets and the resources needed to meet these targets is part of which principal function of management?
   A Controlling
   B Directing
   C Organising
   D Planning

2 Which of the following is **not** one of Fayol's five functions of management?
   A Organising
   B Motivating
   C Commanding
   D Co-ordinating

3 Which of the following roles comes under Mintzberg's category of decisional management?
   A Figurehead
   B Spokesperson
   C Liaison
   D Negotiator

4 Which of the following is a feature of autocratic management?
   A Delegation
   B Two-way communication
   C Quick decision-making
   D Meeting of employees' social needs

5 Which of the following is a belief held by a Theory X manager, according to Douglas McGregor?
   A Workers are only motivated by money.
   B Workers look for job satisfaction.
   C Workers perform badly if work is monotonous.
   D Workers wish to contribute to decision-making.

Exam-style questions: Short answer

1 Explain the difference between management and leadership. [3]

   ....

   ....

2 Explain **one** advantage and **one** disadvantage to a car manufacturing business of increased delegation. [6]

   ....

   ....

   ....

   ....

3 Analyse **two** business situations where laissez-faire management may be appropriate. [8]

   ....

   ....

....

....

....

....

4 Using examples, explain how **two** of Fayol's principles of management may be used by a warehouse
  manager for an online retail company. [6]

....

....

....

....

5 Evaluate the importance of a manager's contribution to the performance of a banking organisation. [12]

....

....

....

....

....

....

....

....

Case study

. . . .

Read the case study and answer the questions on a separate sheet.

Shanthi is the General Manager of the Beach Hotel in a big holiday resort in Bali, Indonesia. She
makes all decisions and manages the teams of workers in all departments, including catering,
housekeeping, reception and finance. Shanthi sets weekly targets for all the departments and
expects team leaders to make sure they are met. Team leaders often leave to join other hotels, as
they feel that they have no say in decision-making and no opportunities to contribute ideas.

1 Define 'management' as a business function. [2]

2 Explain **two** features of an autocratic manager. [6]

3 Explain **two** advantages to the Beach Hotel of Shanthi's management style. [6]

4 With reference to McGregor's Theory X and Y managers, analyse **two** possible reasons for
  Shanthi's management approach. [8]

5 Evaluate whether Shanthi should delegate some decision-making to her department team
  leaders. Justify your recommendation. [12]

3 Marketing

▶ 3.1 The nature of marketing

> **KEY TERMS**
>
> Marketing, corporate and marketing objectives, sales targets, brand awareness, market/consumer/product orientation, demand and supply, market size, market growth, market share, business-to-business marketing (B2B), business-to-consumer marketing (B2C), market segmentation, mass and niche marketing, customer-relationship marketing (CRM).

▶ Multiple choice questions

*Circle the **one** correct answer.*

1 Which of the following would **not** be an aim of the marketing department?
   A To add value
   B To cut costs
   C To create customers
   D To create awareness

2 Which of the following firms would be most likely to use B2B marketing?
   A A supermarket
   B A car showroom
   C A building supplies merchant
   D A fashion clothing company

3 Which type of segmentation identifies customer groups according to their attitudes and lifestyle choices?
   A Demographic
   B Geographic
   C Socio-economic
   D Psychographic

4 Which of the following is a benefit of targeting a niche market?
   A It is a large market with many potential customers.
   B It is easy to target promotional spending.
   C It will always remain a niche market.
   D It will enable lower prices to be charged.

5 Which one of the following will lead to a company achieving its objective of increasing market share?
   A It spends more money on advertising.
   B It sells more products.
   C It attracts customers away from competitors.
   D It decreases prices.

Now try this

How has the internet changed the way that companies market their products? Compare web-based marketing with traditional methods, such as TV and newspapers. What are the advantages and disadvantages of modern methods of marketing to firms and consumers?

Exam-style questions: Short answer

The market for fast food in Brighton, UK

Brighton is a seaside town in the United Kingdom, which attracts tourists all the year round. There are many fast-food outlets and restaurants in the town. A group of students from the local college have been researching the market for fast food in the town and have estimated the following figures, for each type of product:

Table 3.1

	Sales this year ($m)	Predicted sales next year ($m)
Total market size	48.5	55.5
Burger sales	12.5	13
Fried chicken sales	11.5	11.8
Pizza sales	10.2	12.2
Sandwich sales	5.5	8.5

1 Define the term 'market'. [2]

....

....

2 Calculate the predicted percentage market growth for the fast-food market next year. [2]

....

....

3 Using calculations, analyse which fast-food products have a predicted gain in market share and which are predicted to lose market share. [6]

....

....

....

....

4 Max is considering entering the fast-food market in Brighton by starting a vegan sandwich bar. He thinks that this is a niche market and hopes that he will be able to build a loyal customer base from local customers as well as tourists.

Evaluate the importance of customer-relationship marketing to a new business in the fast-food market. [12]

....

....

....

....

....

....

....

▶ 3.2 Market research

KEY TERMS

Market research, primary and secondary research, target population, sample/random/stratified/quota sampling, quantitative and qualitative data, focus group, validity and reliability of data.

▶ Multiple choice questions

*Circle the **one** correct answer.*

1 Which of the following would **not** be a source of primary market research data for a fast-food business?
   A Customer surveys
   B Focus groups
   C Sales figures for previous month
   D Observation of competitor's tactics

2 Which of the following is another term for secondary market research?
   A Desk research
   B First-hand research
   C Internet research
   D Field research

3 A market researcher identifies that she must collect the views of 100 respondents, of whom 30 must be male and 70 female. Which type of sampling is this an example of?
   A Convenience
   B Quota
   C Random
   D Stratified

4 A market researcher sends an internet survey to every fifth customer on his mailing list. Which type of sampling is this an example of?
   A Quota
   B Convenience
   C Stratified
   D Random

5 Which of the following will **not** lead to the collection of qualitative data?
   A A focus group
   B A tickbox survey
   C An interview
   D Consumer feedback forms

Now try this

How has the Internet changed the way that companies market their products? Choose a growing retail company in your country that has a marketing objective to increase market share.

Create a presentation that explains three ways in which the company uses the Internet to help towards meeting this objective.

Exam-style questions: Short answer

The rise and rise of the vegan roll

For companies selling food and snacks, it is essential to keep up with consumer eating trends. The recent increase in consumers choosing to eat a vegan diet is an example of this.

Bob's Snacks is a bakery company in a large city in Europe. Bob observed that a number of customers were asking questions about which of his products were 'vegan-friendly'. He also read an article on an internet news site on the subject. Bob carried out some consumer surveys and discovered that there was, indeed, a significant demand for vegan products. Bob's response to this was to launch a vegan pastry roll. Sales in the first month were incredible; he could hardly keep up with demand. The local newspaper published an interview and a review which increased demand even further. Bob is now developing more vegan snacks to satisfy this growing market.

1 Define the term 'market research'. [2]

....

....

2 Identify the target population for Bob's vegan pastry rolls. [2]

....

....

3 Analyse **two** benefits of the primary and secondary market research that was carried out by Bob. [8]

....

....

....

....

....

....

4 Evaluate the importance of market research to the ongoing success of Bob's vegan snacks. [12]

....

....

....

....

....

....

....

....

▶ **3.3** The marketing mix

KEY TERMS

Marketing mix: the 4Ps (Product, Price, Promotion and Place), tangible and intangible attributes of products, product differentiation and unique selling point (USP), product portfolio analysis, product life cycle and extension strategies, Boston Matrix, pricing methods, competitive pricing, penetration pricing, price skimming, price taking, price discrimination, cost-based pricing, psychological pricing, dynamic pricing, promotional mix, branding, marketing expenditure budget, channel of distribution, internet and the marketing mix.

▶ Multiple choice questions

*Circle the **one** correct answer.*

1 Which of the following would be an intangible attribute of a mobile phone?
   A Wi-Fi connectivity
   B Loaded apps
   C 12-month guarantee
   D Video camera

2 Which of the following describes the sales of a product during the maturity phase of its product life cycle?
   A Sales starting from launch of product
   B Sales increasing fast
   C Sales steady but not growing
   D Sales declining

3 A vegan snack has a high market share in the fast-growing market for vegan food. How would the Boston Matrix categorise this product?
   A Cash cow   C Question mark
   B Dog   D Star

4 A shoe shop prices its products at $10.99, $29.99, $39.99 and $49.99. What pricing method is this an example of?
   A Penetration pricing
   B Psychological pricing
   C Price discrimination
   D Dynamic pricing

5 Which of the following would **not** be included in the promotional mix for a new style of designer trainers?
   A Advertising
   B Branding
   C Packaging
   D Free samples

Now try this

Choose a product that you and/or your family like or buy regularly. Carry out a detailed analysis of each aspect of its marketing mix, focusing on how the elements are integrated (or fit in) with each other. Create a drawn or printed display for your classroom.

Table exercise

Fill in the table to match the example with the pricing method and explain your answer in the right-hand column.

Table 3.2

Example	Pricing method	Description/explanation
A mobile phone company launches a new model at a high price.		
A fashion clothing company collects information about prices charged by other companies for similar items.		
A multinational soft drinks company sells a new flavour of fizzy water at a very low price for the first month.		
A jewellery maker calculates the total cost of producing an item and then adds on a percentage mark-up.		
A train company charges different fares according to the time of purchase and time of travel.		

Exam-style questions: Short answer

The new bicycle tour company

Mike's Bikes is a large bicycle and accessories retailer in a big coastal city in Asia. Mike also rents bicycles out by the day, week or month. The area is popular with tourists, who come to stay in hotels, sight-see and experience markets and other attractions. Sales of bicycles are booming and there are plenty of cycle paths throughout the city.

Mike has had a new idea: he wants to start providing guided bicycle tours. The tours will include meals and tourist attraction entrance fees. Each group will be accompanied by a professional tour guide. There is no similar service being offered at present and Mike thinks that this new venture will be very popular.

Mike has carried out research into similar services in other locations and has worked out the cost of all aspects of the tours, including the guide, meals, bicycles and insurance. Mike knows that most of his customers will be international tourists, staying in the many large hotels in the city.

Mike's brother has designed a new website for the launch of Mike's Bike Tours, which also allows customers to make enquiries and bookings.

1   Define the term 'unique selling point (USP)'. [2]

....

....

2   Analyse **two** aspects of Mike's product portfolio, using the concepts of product life cycle and the Boston Matrix. [8]

....

....

....

....

....

....

3 Analyse **two** methods of pricing which may be suitable for Mike's Bike Tours. [8]

....

....

....

....

....

....

4 The 'place' element of the marketing mix refers to how the product or service may be bought by consumers. Analyse **two** ways that customers might book Mike's bike tours, other than by visiting his shop. [8]

....

....

....

....

....

5 Recommend a promotional plan for the launch of Mike's Bike Tours to international tourists. [12]

....

....

....

....

....

....

....

4 Operations management

▶ 4.1 The nature of operations

> **KEY TERMS**
>
> Operations, production, transformational process, efficiency, effectiveness, labour and capital productivity, inputs/outputs, sustainability, labour-intensive and capital-intensive production, job/batch/flow production, mass customisation, market forces.

▶ Multiple choice questions

*Circle the **one** correct answer.*

1 Which of the following would **not** be an aim of the operations department?
   A To add value
   B To increase efficiency
   C To increase sustainability
   D To decrease productivity

2 Which of the following actions would be most likely to increase productivity in a clothing factory?
   A Employing more workers
   B More training for workers
   C Longer hours for workers
   D Increasing labour turnover

3 Which type of production moves items in groups through the transformation process?
   A Batch production
   B Job production
   C Mass production
   D Flow production

4 Which of the following is a feature of sustainable production?
   A More use of capital equipment
   B More use of recycled packaging
   C More use of non-renewable resources
   D More use of labour

5 Which of the following may be most suitable for production using mass customisation?
   A Cement production
   B Car production
   C Apple production
   D Bread production

Now try this

In groups, discuss the inputs, transformation process and output involved in the production of a basic cheese and tomato pizza.
   » Estimate the cost of ingredients needed to make a batch of ten pizzas.
   » Identify all the steps involved in the transformation process.
   » Estimate the sales revenue made by the pizza company from the sale of ten pizzas.
   » Calculate the total added value from the transformation process.

Draw a diagram in your notes, illustrating this example.

Exam-style questions: Short answer

Good Eggs

Good Eggs is a chicken farm and egg producer. The chickens are kept outdoors and the eggs are categorised as 'free range' and can be sold at a premium price.

The eggs are collected by hand and loaded onto a production line that transports them into the packing shed. Workers take the eggs off the production line and pack them into boxes of six and twelve in sizes small, medium and large. All eggs are stamped with a quality assurance mark.

Zoe, the owner of Good Eggs, is always looking to increase productivity and efficiency. She is considering the purchase of an egg-packing machine. The initial cost of $200 000 would be a major investment, but would automate the final packing process and eliminate the need for the labour involved in that process.

1   Define what is meant by 'efficiency'.   [2]

....

....

2   Identify and explain **one** example of labour-intensive production in the Good Eggs factory.   [3]

....

....

....

3   Analyse **two** ways that Good Eggs adds value during the production process.   [8]

....

....

....

....

....

....

4   Evaluate whether Good Eggs should purchase the egg-packing machine. Justify your recommendation.   [12]

....

....

....

....

....

....

....

....

4.2 Inventory management

KEY TERMS
Inventory, buffer inventory, reorder level, lead time, inventory control, supply chain management, just in time (JIT), just in case (JIC).

Multiple choice questions

*Circle the **one** correct answer.*

1 Which of the following is a reason for keeping buffer inventory?
   A For day-to-day production
   B In case of machine breakdown
   C In case of supply problems
   D For JIT production

2 Which of the following would **not** be an example of inventory held in a clothing factory?
   A Supplies of thread
   B Supplies of finished garments
   C Supplies of partly finished garments
   D Supplies of machine components

3 What is a likely impact of a significant increase in the lead time for delivery of flour to a bread factory that uses JIT inventory control?
   A A build-up of flour inventory
   B A delay in production
   C A decrease in added value
   D An increase in opportunity cost

4 Which of the following is an opportunity cost of holding high levels of inventory in a jewellery shop?
   A Many styles can be kept in inventory
   B Money is tied up in inventory of jewellery
   C More customer needs may be met
   D Cost of inventory may increase

5 Which of the following is a key aim of Just in Time (JIT) inventory management?
   A Cutting down on use of labour
   B Increasing buffer stocks
   C Increasing use of quality control
   D Cutting down on warehousing costs

Now try this

In groups, discuss the inventory control process in a fast-food pizza delivery company. See if you can answer the following questions:
» What information will help the company manager to estimate the amount of inventory she needs to hold?
» Make a list of items, such as ingredients and packaging, that need to be kept as inventory.
» Which items are perishable? Non-perishable?
» Draw an inventory control diagram in your notes, illustrating the inventory control of one ingredient, such as flour or tomato sauce.

Exam-style questions: Short answer

Harry's fish and chips

Harry owns and runs a fish-and-chip takeaway shop in a big town in the USA. Customers order food online or come into the shop and wait. All food is cooked fresh and Harry's unique selling point is that the fish is bought fresh, daily, from the local market. Other ingredients, such as cooking oil and potatoes for the chips, can be stored for a few days. Harry relies on a local food wholesaler to deliver these other ingredients.

Harry tries to buy different fish according to likely demand, but often has inventory left over which is wasted. Sometimes, on a very busy weekend day, Harry runs out of fish and has to disappoint customers.

1 Define what is meant by 'inventory control'. [2]

....

....

2 Identify and explain **one** supplier that Harry relies on to get his inventory. [3]

....

....

....

3 Analyse **one** example of JIT and **one** example of JIC inventory management from Harry's fish-and-chip shop. [8]

....

....

....

....

....

....

4 Evaluate whether Harry should increase his storage space and keep a buffer inventory of frozen fish in his shop. [12]

....

....

....

....

....

....

....

....

▶ 4.3 Capacity utilisation and outsourcing

KEY TERMS
Capacity, capacity utilisation, rationalisation, capacity under-utilisation, capacity over-utilisation, subcontracting, outsourcing, maximum capacity, under maximum capacity, over maximum capacity.

▶ Multiple choice questions

*Circle the **one** correct answer.*

1 Which of the following is **not** a reason for increasing capacity utilisation?
- **A** To decrease unit costs
- **B** To meet increased demand
- **C** To increase fixed costs
- **D** To use resources efficiently

2 A firm has a maximum capacity of 2000 items. Current production level is 1400 items. What is the current capacity utilisation?
- **A** 70%
- **B** 40%
- **C** 30%
- **D** 20%

3 What is a likely solution for a firm facing capacity under-utilisation?
- **A** Increasing capacity
- **B** Outsourcing
- **C** Subcontracting
- **D** Decreasing employees

4 A computer firm has a maximum capacity of 10 000 and current demand for 12 000 units. What is a possible solution to meet this demand?
- **A** Buy more components
- **B** Lower the price
- **C** Outsource part of production
- **D** Increase capacity utilisation

5 Which of the following is a disadvantage to a firm of outsourcing?
- **A** Cutting down pressure on labour
- **B** Decreasing the need to hold inventory
- **C** Allowing all orders to be met
- **D** Having less control over quality

Exam-style questions: Short answer

1 Define the term 'capacity over-utilisation'. [2]

....

....

2 Analyse **one** advantage and **one** disadvantage of working at 90 per cent capacity for a company running a theme park. [8]

....

....

....

....

....

....

3 Evaluate whether a multinational company making tablet computers should outsource part of the production process to an overseas manufacturer. [12]

....

....

....

....

....

....

....

Case study

•••

Read the case study and answer the questions on a separate sheet.

Dasha owns a small clothing manufacturer, located in a developing country. The company makes ready-made garments (RMGs) for designer clothing companies. Production is labour intensive, carried out by 100 employees cutting cloth and sewing in a small factory. Cutting is done by hand and each employee works on a sewing machine to create the garments. Maximum production capacity is 8000 garments per week and the company currently works at between 60 per cent and 85 per cent capacity.

Orders are received from the designer clothing companies on a seasonal basis, so are unpredictable. Dasha is always keen to keep enough capacity available to meet extra or urgent orders. She is considering a new investment into a machine that would help with the cutting of cloth and increase the number of garments that can be produced.

The company has been offered a large order for school uniforms from a famous private school. Subject to satisfactory quality, this could become a regular yearly commitment. Dasha has worked out that she has current capacity to produce all except the school blazers, which are jackets for both boys and girls with the school badge on the top pocket. Dasha would like to accept this order but is trying to decide whether to outsource part of the uniform production or invest in the new cutting machine.

1 Identify how **each** of the four factors of production are used in Dasha's clothing company: land; labour; capital; enterprise. [8]

2 Calculate the number of garments that will be produced weekly, if Dasha's factory works at 60 per cent capacity. [2]

3 Analyse **one** advantage and **one** disadvantage to Dasha's clothing of working at 60 per cent capacity. [8]

4 Evaluate whether Dasha's clothing should outsource production of the school blazers. [12]

5 Finance and accounting

▶ 5.1 Business finance

> **KEY TERMS**
>
> Capital, asset, current assets, need for finance, liabilities, insolvency, bankruptcy, working capital, trade receivables and trade payables, capital expenditure, revenue expenditure, liquidation, administration.

▶ Multiple choice questions

*Circle the **one** correct answer.*

1 Which of the following may lead to business insolvency?
   A Sales revenue greater than variable costs
   B Liabilities greater than assets
   C Increasing need for capital for growth
   D Profit less than previous year

2 When a limited company fails, which of the following is **not** a result?
   A Insolvency
   B Administration
   C Liquidation
   D Bankruptcy

3 A business has $2500 cash in the bank and stock worth $6000. It owes $300 to suppliers and has an outstanding bank loan of $5000. What is the value of its working capital?
   A $8500
   B $8200
   C $3500
   D $3200

4 Which of the following is **not** an example of capital expenditure for a supermarket?
   A Paying for a self-scanning system
   B Paying for a new shelving unit
   C Paying for new shop flooring
   D Paying for a marketing campaign

Exam-style questions: Short answer

1 What is the difference between an asset and a liability? [2]

....

....

2 Using examples, explain **two** reasons why a small business may require finance. [6]

....

....

....

....

3 Analyse **two** reasons why it is important for a business to monitor its trade receivables and trade payables.
[8]

....

....

....

....

....

....

4 Explain, using **two** examples, the difference between capital expenditure and revenue expenditure for a chicken-farming business.
[6]

....

....

....

....

5 Evaluate the view that 'cash is more important than profit to a growing business'.
[12]

....

....

....

....

....

....

....

....

Case study

· ·

Read the case study and answer the questions on a separate sheet.

Ruth was full of optimism when she opened her new cake shop as a sole trader business. She had invested her savings of $20 000 and taken a bank loan of $40 000 to start the business. Ruth felt that her business had gone well during the early months of trading. However, many of her business customers, who bought goods on credit, were slow to pay. Ruth had made sure she paid her suppliers promptly, in order to build up good relationships. However, after six months, Ruth was worried that she might go bankrupt.

1   Identify and explain **one** example of a non-current liability from the case study.   [3]

2   State **one** example of a trade payable and **one** example of a trade receivable from the case study.   [2]

3   Explain **two** reasons why Ruth may have given business customers the opportunity to buy goods on credit.   [6]

4   Analyse **two** possible reasons why Ruth's business may go bankrupt.   [8]

5   Evaluate how Ruth may try to ensure the survival of her business. Justify your recommendation.   [12]

▶ 5.2 Sources of finance

KEY TERMS

Internal and external sources of finance, bank loan, share capital, bank overdraft, trade credit, leasing and hire purchase, mortgage, debenture, venture capital, debt factoring, microfinance, crowdfunding, government grant, rate of interest, non-current assets.

▶ Multiple choice questions

1   Which of the following would **not** be a suitable source of finance for a sole trader start-up business?
    A   Crowdfunding
    B   Bank loan
    C   Sale of shares
    D   Owner's savings

2   Which of the following would be categorised as an external source of finance?
    A   Sale of assets
    B   Working capital
    C   Retained earnings
    D   Trade credit

3   Which of the following could be purchased by a soft drinks company using a mortgage as a source of finance?
    A   A new factory
    B   A company van
    C   A bottling machine
    D   A new computer system

4   Which of the following is **not** a benefit of debt factoring to a private limited company?
    A   The company gets paid the full amount owed.
    B   The company's overdraft charges may be lower.
    C   The company receives cash quickly.
    D   The company can pay its own outstanding bills.

5   A small entrepreneur sources finance for a high-risk new product idea, in return for giving another organisation a share of the company. What is this an example of?
    A   Sale of shares
    B   Venture capital
    C   Crowdfunding
    D   Microfinance

6   Which of the following is an example of a short-term source of finance?
    A   A mortgage
    B   A government grant
    C   Share capital
    D   An overdraft

Table exercise

Consider the example scenarios in Table 5.1 on the next page and suggest the most suitable source(s) of finance. Remember that businesses often use several sources to finance a project. Justify your choice in the right-hand column, including any disadvantages.

Table 5.1

Scenario	Source(s) of finance	Why is it suitable? (Include advantages and disadvantages.)
A new entrepreneur has $40 000 in savings, but needs an extra $30 000 to start a bicycle repair business.		
A social enterprise wants to expand a recycling project in a developing country.		
A popular online author has a good idea for a self-help book, which will cost $25 000 to publish.		
A large, public limited fast-food company wants to take over a competitor at a cost of $50 million.		
A global pharmaceutical company is carrying out research into a new vaccine for a serious virus and needs $30 million.		
A private limited company in the retail fashion industry wants to expand throughout the country.		

Exam-style questions: Short answer

1 Define the term 'internal sources of finance'. [2]

....

....

2 Explain **two** advantages to a private limited company that manufactures solar energy products of using a government grant to develop a mobile phone charger. [6]

....

....

....

....

3 Analyse **two** disadvantages to a public limited company of raising finance through an issue of new shares on the stock exchange. [8]

....

....

....

....

....

....

4 Explain, using **one** example, how a hotel business might use sale and leaseback of non-current assets as a source of finance. [3]

....

....

....

5 Evaluate the importance of the availability of microfinance to small entrepreneurs in a developing country. [12]

....

....

....

....

....

....

....

....

Case study

Read the case study and answer the questions on a separate sheet.

Aron and Cara own a successful partnership business, which they started using their own savings. They source, process and sell spices for cooking. Their customers are retailers and also manufacturers of 'ready meals'. The partnership is profitable, but retained earnings are very low as all the profits have been reinvested into the business or used as income by the partners. Aron and Cara agree that they would like to expand and produce their own range of cooking sauces. However, they disagree on the best way to finance the $500 000 required. Aron would like to take on a new partner, but Cara thinks they should convert the business to a private limited company and invite family and friends to invest.

1 Define the term 'retained earnings'. [2]

2 Identify and explain **one** reason why Aron and Cara's own savings were a suitable source of start-up finance for their spice business. [3]

3 Explain **one** advantage and **one** disadvantage to Aron and Cara of reinvesting most of their profit into the business. [6]

4 Analyse **two** sources of finance that the partners could consider for their new cooking sauces, other than those suggested in the case study. [8]

5 Evaluate how Aron and Cara should finance their business growth. Justify your recommendation. [12]

▶ 5.3 Forecasting and managing cash flows

KEY TERMS

Cash, cash flow, cash inflow, cash outflow, cash-flow forecast, cash sales, credit sales, short-term borrowing, sale and leaseback of assets, opening balance, closing balance.

▶ Multiple choice questions

*Circle the **one** correct answer.*

1 Which of the following is **not** an example of a cash inflow for a new business?
   A Credit sales
   B Cash in the bank
   C Employee wages
   D Owner's savings

2 A business has an opening balance of $1500. It makes sales of $800, pays $200 for raw materials and $500 for wages. Calculate its closing balance.
   A $1000   C $1500
   B $100   D $1600

3 Which of the following would **not** be a suitable solution for a forecast negative cash flow?
   A Faster payment of trade payables
   B Faster payment of trade receivables
   C Debt factoring
   D A bank overdraft

4 Which of the following is a benefit to a business of drawing up a cash-flow forecast?
   A It may help to collect trade receivables.
   B It guarantees a positive cash flow.
   C It shows forecast profit.
   D It may help to apply for a loan.

5 Which of the following would be categorised as cash in a business?
   A Profit
   B Trade receivables
   C Funds in the bank
   D Trade payables

Exam-style questions: Short answer

Marie's sandwich bar

The questions are based on the following cash-flow forecast for Marie's new sandwich shop. She has drawn this up to cover her first four months after opening. Marie has included her cash flow forecast in her business plan.

Table 5.2 Cash-flow forecast for Marie's sandwich bar

	April	May	June	July
Cash in				
Start-up loan	$15000			
Owner's savings	$12000			
Cash sales	$ 2000	$3000	$3000	$4000
Credit sales			$2000	$2000
Total cash inflow				
Cash out				
Shop fitting and equipment	$25000			
Rent	$ 1000	$1000	$1000	$1000
Raw materials (ingredients)	$ 1000	$1250	$1250	$1500
Wages	$ 1500	$1500	$1500	$1500

	April	May	June	July
Marketing	$ 300	$ 50	$ 50	$ 50
Loan repayment	$ 500	$ 500	$ 500	$ 500
Total cash outflow				
Net monthly cash flow				
Opening balance	$ 0			
Closing balance				

Credit sales are made to a local company who order sandwiches for meetings. Marie has allowed the company 60 days' credit.

1 Define the term 'cash flow'. [2]

....

....

2 Calculate the figures for total cash inflow, total cash outflow, net monthly cash flow, opening balance and closing balance for all four months, and enter them into the table above. [8]

3 Analyse **two** ways in which Marie might try to improve her forecast cash-flow position for May and June. [8]

....

....

....

....

....

....

4 Using Marie's cash-flow forecast as an example, evaluate the view that 'cash flow is not the same as profit'. [12]

....

....

....

....

....

....

▶ **5.4** Costs

KEY TERMS

Costs, revenue, break-even, fixed costs, variable costs, total costs, profit, direct costs, indirect costs, overheads, marginal cost, average cost, full/absorption costing, contribution, contribution costing and pricing, cost-plus pricing, budgets, special-order decisions, break-even chart, margin of safety.

▶ Multiple choice questions

*Circle the **one** correct answer.*

1 Which of the following is **not** a reason why businesses need accurate cost information?
  A To help in predicting break-even output
  B To help in making business start-up decisions
  C To help in predicting sales
  D To help in deciding whether to accept a special order

2 Which of the following is another name for an indirect cost?
  A Variable cost
  B Overhead cost
  C Marginal cost
  D Average cost

3 Which of the following would be a direct cost for a fast-food burger café?
  A Burger buns
  B Employee wages
  C Shop rent
  D Cleaning cost

4 Which of the following is a definition of a marginal cost?
  A The variable cost of one unit produced
  B The fixed costs divided by the number of units
  C The total cost divided by the number of units
  D The amount added to total cost by production of one more unit

5 A break-even chart does **not** include which of the following lines?
  A Total revenue
  B Total profit
  C Total fixed costs
  D Total costs

Table exercise

It is vital that you learn the formula for each type of cost and related concepts, such as break-even. You will then be able to apply these to case study scenarios. Copy and fill in the table below with definitions and formulae, before answering the rest of the questions.

Table 5.3

Cost/concept	Definition/description	Formula (if applicable)
Fixed (or indirect) costs, also known as overheads		
Variable (or direct) cost		
Total variable (or direct) costs		
Total revenue		
Profit		
Total costs		
Average cost		
Marginal cost		

Cost/concept	Definition/description	Formula (if applicable)
Contribution per unit		
Total contribution		
Break-even output		
Margin of safety		

Exam-style questions: Short answer

1 Define the term 'variable costs'. [2]

....

....

2 Explain **two** advantages to a multi-product clothing production company of using the full- or absorption-costing method. [6]

....

....

....

....

3 Analyse **two** difficulties for the clothing company in question 2 when trying to allocate indirect costs between five different production lines. [8]

....

....

....

....

....

4 Explain, using **one** example, how a sandwich shop might use cost-plus pricing for its ready-made sandwiches. [3]

....

....

....

....

5 Evaluate whether the use of cost-plus pricing might guarantee that the company in question 4 makes a profit. [12]

....

....

....

....

....

....

....

....

Case study

Read the case study and answer the questions on a separate sheet. You will need graph or squared paper for the break-even chart.

Winnie is managing director of a small company that produces solar-powered lamps and phone chargers. She buys small solar panels in bulk from her supplier and her employees manufacture the lamps and chargers in a small factory.

Table 5.4 Financial data for solar lamps and phone chargers ($)

Product	Solar lamp	Solar phone charger
Bought-in solar panel per unit	$ 3.00	$3.00
Other components per unit	$ 3.00	$2.00
Labour cost per unit	$ 2.50	$1.50
Selling price per unit	$12.00	$9.00
Contribution per unit	X	Y
Maximum output capacity per month	1500	2000
Current monthly output	1000	1800
Factory total indirect costs per month	7000	

1 Define the term 'indirect costs'. [2]

2 Calculate contribution per unit for the solar lamps and phone chargers (X and Y in the table). [2]

3 Use graph or squared paper. Assuming that Winnie decides to allocate $3000 of indirect costs to the solar lamp production line, draw a break-even chart showing break-even monthly output and the margin of safety at the current monthly output. [14]

4 Winnie has received a special order from a social enterprise for 300 solar phone chargers, for use by volunteers in a charity project. They will need to be delivered in one month. The customer will pay a price of $7.50 each. Evaluate whether Winnie should accept this order and justify your recommendation. [12]

5.5 Budgets

KEY TERMS
Variance analysis, adverse and favourable variances, incremental budget, flexible budget, zero budget, budget holder.

Multiple choice questions

*Circle the **one** correct answer.*

1 Which of the following would **not** be included in an expenditure budget?
  A Rent
  B Wages
  C Credit sales
  D Overheads

2 Which of the following would lead to a favourable variance?
  A Cash sales lower than forecast
  B Overheads higher than forecast
  C Marketing costs higher than forecast
  D Material costs lower than forecast

3 Which of the following describes the process of incremental budgeting?
  A Budgeting based on a percentage change to previous year's budget
  B Budgeting justified by planned item expenditure
  C Budgeting based on a set amount given to each department
  D Budgeting that changes according to sales volume

4 Which of the following is a benefit of zero budgets?
  A It helps to set a sales revenue budget.
  B It guarantees that spending will not exceed budget.
  C It allocates more spending to managers who are skilled negotiators.
  D It helps firms divert spending to the most important functions.

5 Which of the following would **not** be a budgeting response to an adverse sales budget variance at the end of one month?
  A Adjust the materials budget downwards
  B Adjust the profit budget downwards
  C Adjust the wages budget upwards
  D Adjust the marketing budget upwards

Now try this

How might you plan a budget for an event such as a party or enterprise activity at school?

Discuss how you would plan expenditure on each different item. Discuss whether making a budget would stop you from overspending.

What might be the disadvantages of this use of budgets?

Exam-style questions: Short answer
Tomo's Taxis
The questions are based on the following three-month budget for Tomo's Taxis. He has drawn this up using a zero-budgeting approach.

Table 5.5 Three-month budget for Tomo's Taxis

	Budget figure ($)	Actual figure ($)	Variance ($)	Adverse or favourable?
Sales revenue	20000	18000		
Car lease costs	1500	1500		
Fuel costs	4000	3800		
Labour costs (drivers)	6000	5800		
Profit				

1 What is meant by a 'budget'? [2]

....

....

2 In the table above, fill in the figures for variances, whether they are adverse or favourable and the budget, actual, and variance data for Tomo's profit. [8]

3 Analyse **two** reasons for the variances in fuel costs, labour costs and profit. [8]

....

....

....

....

....

....

4 Using Tomo's budget as an example, evaluate the view that 'setting a budget will ensure that a business does not overspend'. [12]

....

....

....

....

....

....

....

Business and its environment

▶ 6.1 External influences on business activity

6.1.1 Political and legal

KEY TERMS

External influences, political and legal environment, privatisation, nationalisation, innovation, public interest, employment practices, conditions of work, wage levels, minimum wage, consumer protection law, competition law, competition and markets authority (CMA), business location law, laws controlling the sale of particular goods and services.

▶ True/false questions

● ●

Decide whether each of the statements below is true or false. Circle the correct answer and explain your decision. Use an example from a business you have learnt about if appropriate.

1 External influences are those factors that a business can control. [3]

True/False

....

....

....

2 Privatisation of state-owned businesses will often lead to greater efficiency. [3]

True/False

....

....

....

3 Employment laws only benefit employees. [3]

True/False

....

....

....

4 Governments try to protect consumers from misleading claims in advertising. [3]

True/False

....

....

....

5 Businesses with dominant market share (more than 25 per cent) always exploit consumers. [3]

True/False

....

....

....

Research task

Do this individually or in small groups.

Research the laws that the government in your country uses to protect employees and consumers. Produce a leaflet about this, with illustrations, aimed at new start-up entrepreneurs. Make sure that you explain the laws in easy-to-understand language.

6.1.2 Economic

KEY TERMS

Economic influences, infrastructure, policies to encourage enterprise, regulation, taxation and subsidy, market failure, collusion, monopolies and cartels, macroeconomic objectives, economic growth, inflation, unemployment, exchange rate, level of economic activity, recession, slump, recovery, boom, business or trade cycle, demand-pull and cost-push inflation, consumer price index (CPI), cyclical/frictional/structural unemployment, currency appreciation and depreciation, monetary/fiscal/supply side/exchange rate policy, direct and indirect taxes.

▶ True/false questions

Decide whether each of the statements below is true or false. Circle the correct answer and explain your decision. Use an example from a business you have learnt about if appropriate.

1 Governments in most countries worldwide encourage enterprise and new business start-ups. [3]

True/False

....

....

....

2 An example of market failure is when a business causes pollution and does not pay to
   clean it up.   [3]

   True/False

   ....

   ....

   ....

3 High inflation is a macroeconomic objective of governments.   [3]

   True/False

   ....

   ....

   ....

4 Demand-pull inflation is high during a recession.   [3]

   True/False

   ....

   ....

   ....

5 Currency appreciation in a country makes its imports and exports cheaper.   [3]

   True/False

   ....

   ....

   ....

Research task

Do this individually or in small groups.

Choose six countries worldwide on different continents, including developed and developing countries. Research their economic indicators (economic growth, inflation and unemployment) and create a table displaying this information. Write a short report comparing the indicators, identifying differences and similarities and any correlation between the rates of growth, inflation and unemployment.

6.1.3–7 Other

KEY TERMS

Social factors, demographic change, technological/international/environmental factors, competitors and suppliers, pressure group, social auditing, sustainable production, social accounting, demography, migration, urbanisation, market structure, disruptive innovation, trade openness, the internet of things (IoT), blockchain, 3-D printing, artificial intelligence (AI), multinational companies, environmental audit.

► True/false questions

•••

Decide whether each of the statements below is true or false. Circle the correct answer and explain your decision. Use an example from a business you have learnt about if appropriate.

1 An aging population means that there will be a higher percentage of young people in future years. [3]

   True/False

   ....

   ....

   ....

2 Introduction of computerised technology in manufacturing decreases total costs. [3]

   True/False

   ....

   ....

   ....

3 Clothing manufacturing businesses that take account of corporate social responsibility often face higher production costs. [3]

   True/False

   ....

   ....

   ....

4 Technological innovation has developed new markets, products and processes. [3]

   True/False

   ....

   ....

   ....

5 All business organisations need to take account of competitors. [3]

   True/False

   ....

   ....

   ....

6 The entry of a multi-national company always brings benefits to a host country, its citizens and government. [3]

True/False

....

....

....

Research task

Do this individually or in small groups.

Research the concept of 'disruptive innovation'. Create a presentation explaining the concept, with examples of recent developments in the retail industry. Conclude your presentation with your own ideas about the impact of increased use of artificial intelligence (AI).

The Our World theme park

This case study and questions covers all three sections of Chapter 6.1: External influences on business activity.

The Our World (OW) theme park is a joint venture between two large multinational IT companies as part of their commitment to corporate social responsibility (CSR). It is situated in a southern state in the USA, where there are many other visitor attractions. The general manager of OW is Alice King, who has responsibility for its everyday operations and overall budget provided by the joint venture partners.

OW offers visitors a wide range of rides and experiences with an environmental theme, designed by an enthusiastic team of developers. The OW mission statement to 'entertain and educate' makes the park popular with families and school groups. Fifty per cent of visitors to OW are also visitors to the USA on holiday from other countries.

Over recent years, the US dollar has appreciated against most major currencies and economic growth is recovering from a recent recession. Unemployment is falling and inflation is stable at 3 per cent per year. The USA has an aging population, as do many of the other countries where OW visitors come from, including Europe.

OW relies on innovative technology for its rides and experiences, many of which are designed to give visitors the experience of being in remote parts of the world, deep in the oceans and even viewing the planet from a space rocket. Rides are replaced or updated on a very regular basis, to maintain visitor interest and in order to compete with other nearby attractions.

The OW theme park is on the boarder of a large nature reserve containing many endangered species. Although Alice works hard to minimise the impact that the visitor attraction has on the surrounding environment, local pressure groups often complain. They are unhappy about the road improvements that allow access to the park and the increased traffic and queues on busy days.

Once in the park, visitors can download a smartphone app to check on ride queues, book meals and even reserve souvenirs from the shop. Alice is convinced that OW is a sustainable business that will carry on educating and entertaining for many years to come.

The OW theme park rides and associated technology are mainly imported from countries in Southeast Asia. This is possible due to the free trade agreements between the USA and most countries where these resources come from. Recently, there have been signs that the USA may introduce protectionist trade policies, which is a worry for the joint venture partners.

Discussion point

What are the most important external influences impacting businesses in your country at present? Would these influences be positive or negative for a local visitor attraction?

Exam-style questions: Case study

1   Analyse the likely impact of **two** social and demographic factors from the case study on the number of
    visitors to the OW theme park.   [8]

    ....

    ....

    ....

    ....

    ....

    ....

2   Evaluate the importance of corporate social responsibility and social auditing to the joint venture
    partner companies who finance the OW theme park.   [12]

    ....

    ....

    ....

    ....

    ....

    ....

    ....

    ....

    ....

3   Evaluate the likely impact of the economic factors in the case study on the revenue from visitors to
    the OW theme park.   [12]

    ....

    ....

    ....

    ....

    ....

    ....

    ....

4 Analyse **two** likely impacts on OW of the increasing interest in environmental awareness among young people. [8]

....

....

....

....

....

....

5 Evaluate the best way for OW to deal with complaints from pressure groups about the impact of traffic on the nature reserve. [12]

....

....

....

....

....

....

....

6 Evaluate whether continued advances in computer technology will be the most important factor for the future success of the OW theme park. [12]

....

....

....

....

....

....

....

7 Analyse **two** advantages to OW of the free trade agreements between USA and countries in Southeast Asia. [8]

....

....

....

....

....

....

8 Evaluate the possible impact on future business decision-making for OW, if the USA introduces protectionist trade policies. [12]

....

....

....

....

....

....

....

▶ **6.2** Business strategy

Developing business strategy

KEY TERMS

Business strategy, strategic management, analysis/choice/implementation, SWOT analysis, PEST analysis, red and blue ocean strategy, scenario planning, Porter's Five Forces analysis, core competencies analysis, Ansoff Matrix, Force Field Analysis, decision trees.

Table exercise

The key terms listed above are all techniques that support the development of business strategy. In order to use these techniques in a range of scenarios, you need to understand the principles behind each technique and why each one may be more or less useful in any given situation.

The table below shows the three stages of the strategic management process: analysis, choice and implementation. Copy the table and then write the name of each technique under the stage(s) it helps with.

Table 6.1

Analysis	Choice	Implementation

Exam-style questions

1 Evaluate how a large supermarket company might use SWOT and PEST analysis in order to make a successful expansion overseas. [12]

....

....

....

....

....

....

....

....

2 Evaluate why a hotel business might use blue ocean strategy, rather than concentrating on red ocean strategy. [12]

....

....

....

....

....

....

....

....

3 Evaluate how a fast-food company might use Porter's Five Forces analysis to identify changes to the market environment in which they operate. [12]

....

....

....

....

....

....

....

4 Evaluate whether a retail clothing business without identifiable core competencies might fail in the market in your country. [12]

....

....

....

....

....

....

....

5 Evaluate how a wheat-farming business might use the Ansoff Matrix and decision-tree analysis to decide whether to move into chicken farming or use the land to build and rent holiday accommodation to tourists. [12]

....

....

....

....

....

....

....

Corporate planning and implementation

> **KEY TERMS**
> Corporate plan, power/role/task/person/change culture, managing change, transformational leadership, contingency planning, crisis management.

Exam-style questions

1 Evaluate how a computer games company might use a corporate plan when looking to increase its market share. [12]

....

....

....

....

....

....

....

....

2 Evaluate the importance of encouraging a change culture in an international airline business. [12]

....

....

....

....

....

....

....

....

3 Evaluate the importance of a transformational leader to manage change in a newly privatised, large
   electricity supply company.   [12]

....

....

....

....

....

....

....

....

4 Evaluate how the aims and values in the vision/mission statement of a multinational fast-food organisation
   may be reflected in its corporate plan.   [12]

....

....

....

....

....

....

....

5 Evaluate how a large banking business may use contingency planning to try to reduce the chances of
   business failure.   [12]

....

....

....

....

....

....

....

....

The Eco-tourism Group

Yannick inherited his family farm and guest house in 1999 and he remains the managing director of the Eco-tourism Group of hotels (EG). When Yannick took over EG, it was a traditional farm, supplying organic fruit and vegetables to the retail and hotel business on a large, tropical holiday island. The business also included a small guest house, offering basic tourist accommodation to guests – mainly students, who wanted to stay on the popular island at a budget price.

As a university graduate with a degree in tourism and several years' work experience, Yannick could see great potential in the business. Yannick analysed the current business and noted strengths in organic produce and an excellent location, but lack of quality and space in the furnishings and facilities of the guest house. His research into the market concluded that there was an opportunity to offer sustainable, 'ecologically friendly' tourism services, as an alternative to the large hotels. He found out that his eco-tourism hotel idea would attract international tourists with high incomes who were interested in nature and environmental protection. Yannick also found out that the countries where most tourists came from had growing economies and that competition in the airline industry was leading to lower fares.

The years 2000–07 were very successful for Yannick and EG, as he exploited the new niche market. First, Yannick enlarged and upgraded the guest house and introduced a 'personalised customer service' based culture. He also opened a restaurant in the guest house, with a chef famous for his use of local ingredients and recipes. He teamed up with a tourism agency offering a wide choice of land- and sea-based excursions, focused on conservation. In 2005, Yannick had the chance to take over the large Sunny Beach hotel on a nearby island, due to the retirement of the owner. He took a loan from the bank, bought the business and set about managing the change from mass-market tourism to the EG eco-tourism business model.

Yannick has proved himself to be an inspirational leader. He involved all EG employees in the implementation of the new EG vision: 'sustainable tourism, better for all'. The Sunny Beach hotel employees were unhappy about the change, following the EG takeover, but Yannick went to great trouble to speak to everyone personally to reassure them that jobs were safe, and introduced a programme of employee training. This enabled employees who were interested in becoming more involved in decision-making and personalised customer service to thrive. Others, who preferred the autocratic management style of the previous owner, chose to leave the business.

The business went from strength to strength as world interest in environmental issues and eco-tourism increased. EG gained an excellent reputation for quality and many loyal customers, who were happy to pay premium prices for their individually tailored holidays. However, in 2008, the world faced a financial crisis and the years from 2009–11 were very difficult. Yannick had to reduce the size of his workforce due to falling demand, but decided not to look for new markets as he was sure that business would recover. He was correct in this respect, and the years from 2012 saw recovery and further growth in the business. Yannick was able to add a third eco-tourism hotel to the group.

Then, in early 2020, disaster struck. A worldwide virus pandemic led to the complete shutdown of air travel and all tourism. Yannick was forced to close all three hotels and tell most of his employees that he was unsure when or if he would be able to give them work again. In his communication to employees, he said: 'we have plans for some harmful events, such as damage caused by bad weather, but we could not have planned for this economic shock'. Yannick also made regular contact with his loyal customers, explaining how EG was responding to the crisis and keeping the eco-hotels well maintained, ready to welcome them back in the near future.

Yannick is now planning a strategy for the re-opening of his eco-tourism hotels.

Exam-style questions: Case study

1 Evaluate Yannick's business strategy for the growth of EG from 2000–19. [20]

....

....

....

....

....

....

....

....

....

....

....

....

2 Advise on possible business strategies for Yannick to use for the recovery of the EG business, following the global pandemic. Justify your recommendations. [20]

....

....

....

....

....

....

....

....

....

....

....

....

Human resource management

▶ **7.1** Organisational structure

KEY TERMS

Organisational structure, responsibility, levels of hierarchy, span of control, chain of command, centralisation/ decentralisation, functional structure, matrix structure, delayering, trust, tall and flat organisational structures, knowledge management, line and staff managers.

▶ **True/false questions**

Decide whether each of the statements below is true or false. Circle the correct answer and explain your decision. Use an example from a business you have learnt about if appropriate.

1 A middle manager in a large business has both authority and accountability.　[3]

True/False

....

....

....

2 Successful businesses have inflexible organisation structures.　[3]

True/False

....

....

....

3 Empowerment in a business is likely to encourage intrapreneurship.　[3]

True/False

....

....

....

4 Flattening a tall organisational structure is likely to lead to narrower spans of control.　[3]

True/False

....

....

....

5 Decentralisation should lead to greater empowerment of employees. [3]

True/False

....

....

....

Research task

● ●

Work individually or in small groups.

Research a large organisation that you know well. This could be your school or college or a well-known national business, such as a large retail organisation.

Using a large sheet of paper (or electronically), draw an organisation structure, annotating your diagram to show examples of levels of hierarchy, spans of control, chains of command, and identify the type of structure. Also, give examples of individuals who have responsibility, authority and accountability.

▶ **7.2** Business communication

KEY TERMS

Communication, feedback, spoken (verbal)/written communication, electronic communication, visual communication, one-way/two-way communication, vertical/horizontal communication, communication channels, barriers to communication, formal/informal communication.

▶ True/false questions

● ●

Decide whether each of the statements below is true or false. Circle the correct answer and explain your decision. Use an example from a business you have learnt about if appropriate.

1 All communication within a business requires feedback. [3]

True/False

....

....

....

2 Advertising on a website is an example of business communication. [3]

True/False

....

....

....

3 A text message is an example of formal communication.   [3]

   True/False

   ....

   ....

   ....

4 Vertical communication takes place between two employees at the same level of the company
   hierarchy.   [3]

   True/False

   ....

   ....

   ....

5 Use of electronic communication can be both an advantage and a disadvantage to a business
   and its employees.   [3]

   True/False

   ....

   ....

   ....

Research task

Do this individually or in small groups.

Create a presentation, with examples, about the importance of effective business communication,
addressing the following points:
>> Why is effective communication with employees important?
>> How has the use of electronic communication made it easier for a business to promote its
   products to consumers?
>> When might formal communication be important? (**Clue:** Presenting a business plan to a lender
   or holding a company presentation about a new product.)

Kazim's Stores

Kazim and his family own a chain of 40 small convenience stores in one of the mega-cities in Asia. Kazim started as a sole trader in 1997 with one store and has grown the business by reinvesting profit. The business is now a private limited company, and the 20 shareholders are members of Kazim's family. Kazim has always been ambitious and growth, both nationally and internationally, is an important objective for him.

The current organisational structure of Kazim's Stores (KS) is hierarchical. Kazim, as managing director, has formed his management team with four assistant directors, each one in overall charge of a functional area: sales and marketing, premises, inventory control and human resources. Each of the 40 KS stores has a manager, assistant manager, two supervisors and around 10 other employees, who have shop assistant roles. KS has a reputation for excellent customer service and the stores have many loyal customers.

Decision-making is mainly carried out by Kazim and his directors, with the shop managers having authority to make some small local decisions, such as the recruitment of shop assistants. Kazim likes to control the range of products sold and all marketing is done centrally, through the KS website and social media. Kazim and his assistant directors also select new store managers. Most communication to shop managers is one-way and weekly targets are set by email. Kazim and his directors try to visit each store every week, in order to carry out a regular check on standards. However, this has become difficult as the company has grown and traffic has become more congested.

Competition in the retail food market has grown in recent years and many KS stores are now challenged by big multinational supermarkets. Some KS managers have also left the business to join these new companies, as they want more authority and the chance to be involved in decision-making. Some also complain about 'email overload'. This has led to a rise in the rate of staff turnover.

KS now has an opportunity to grow externally, by taking over a similar company, Quality Stores (QS), that operates 30 convenience stores in another city 500 kilometres away. The stores will be rebranded with the KS logo and will sell all the same products as the original stores, once the takeover is complete.

Kazim has held a meeting with his assistant directors to discuss the staff turnover problem and present the proposed expansion. The management team are all agreed on one thing: that the organisational structure of KS and the way stores are managed needs to change, both for the existing stores and in respect of the new stores. Kazim has asked his assistant directors to consider the following questions and bring responses to the next meeting:

» How can KS maintain a high standard of customer service without close monitoring of shops by the management team?
» How might managers of KS stores be delegated sufficient authority to keep them motivated to stay with the business?
» How might KS organise and communicate within the new structure, including the 30 new stores, once the takeover of QS is complete?
» How might a new structure be designed to accommodate international growth in the future?

Discussion point

If you were a member of Kazim's management team, how would you respond to these questions?

Exam-style questions: Case study

1 Analyse **one** advantage and **one** disadvantage of the current organisational structure of KS. [8]

....

....

....

....

....

2 Evaluate whether KS should delegate more authority to its managers. Justify your recommendation. [12]

....

....

....

....

....

....

....

....

3 Evaluate a new organisational structure for KS, following the takeover of QS. Justify your recommendation. [12]

....

....

....

....

....

....

....

....

4 Analyse **two** barriers to communication that KS may experience at it expands nationally and internationally. [8]

....

....

....

....

....

....

5 Evaluate the best way to overcome these barriers. Justify your recommendation. [12]

....

....

....

....

....

....

....

....

6 Evaluate whether improving the effectiveness of communication will be the most important factor for the future success of KS. [12]

....

....

....

....

....

....

....

....

....

....

▶ 7.3 Leadership

KEY TERMS

Trait/behavioural/contingency theory, power and influence theory, transformational theory, delegation, emotional intelligence.

▶ True/false questions

Decide whether each of the statements below is true or false. Circle the correct answer and explain your decision. Use an example from a business you have learnt about if appropriate.

1 Leadership is the same as management. [3]

True/False

....

....

....

2 Trait theory of leadership suggests that a good leader should have charisma. [3]

True/False

....

....

....

3 A good leader in a modern organisation needs to be flexible and able to flourish in a changing environment. [3]

True/False

....

....

....

4 A successful transformational leader will need to have a high level of emotional intelligence (EI). [3]

True/False

....

....

5 A leader must have emotional intelligence in order to inspire employees. [3]

True/False

....

....

....

Research task

Work on this individually or in small groups.

Consider Goleman's four competencies of emotional intelligence: self-awareness, self-management, social awareness and social skills.

Create a poster or PowerPoint presentation which explains how developing each of these competencies may help a person become a transformational leader. (It may help to include examples of situations where the competencies may help to inspire others or solve problems.)

▶ 7.4 Human resource management strategy

> **KEY TERMS**
> Hard and soft approaches to HRM, flexible workforce, temporary workers, annualised hours contract, part-time workers, job-sharing, zero-hours contract, core/peripheral workers, flexitime, shift-working, compressed hours, gig economy, homeworking, on-the-job/off-the-job training, corporate objectives, management by objectives (MBO), performance management.

▶ True/false questions

Decide whether each of the statements below is true or false. Circle the correct answer and explain your decision. Use an example from a business you have learnt about if appropriate.

1 Soft HRM will always improve the productivity of workers. [3]

True/False

....

....

....

2 Leaders who use a hard HRM approach often have a Theory Y view of the workforce. [3]

True/False

....

....

....

3 A flexible workforce usually leads to lower total wage costs for a business. [3]

True/False

....

....

....

4 Workers in the gig economy benefit from regular hours and a stable weekly wage. [3]

True/False

....

....

....

5 Management by objectives means setting one common goal for all members of the
   organisation.   [3]

   True/False

   ....

   ....

   ....

Now try this
• •

Write your answers on a separate sheet.

A specialist bicycle manufacturing company has an average of 150 employees. Last year, the level
of production was 33 400 bicycles. During this same time period, 45 workers left the company
and the average daily absence was 21 workers. Review the formulae for labour productivity, labour
turnover and absenteeism and calculate them for the company. What other information would you
need to judge this company's employee performance?

Case study: Leadership and human resource management: JS Airways

Jo Swift founded JS Airways (JSA) during the 1970s in the UK, as part of his holiday business. The company
became a public limited company in 1997. Jo was a charismatic, 'larger than life' character and had a strong
belief in his principles of 'providing affordable flights and holidays for all'. The airline grew very fast and was
soon challenging major carriers on routes to the USA as well as throughout Europe.

Jo always believed that the key to business success lies with employees. SA pilots, cabin crew and office
workers enjoyed permanent contracts, generous benefits and good salaries, as well as a very comprehensive
training programme. Jo spent much of his time out and about in the office and on flights, making sure that
he was seen as accessible. He was always open to suggestions from employees and offered rewards for ideas
that would make the business more efficient. SA's approach to staff earned the company a reputation as an
excellent employer and there was never a shortage of job applicants.

Jo retired in 2005, just as the 'low-cost' airline business started to become more competitive, due to market
deregulation by European governments. The board of directors appointed a new CEO, Maxine Smith, who was
given the brief to 'cut costs and make SA more competitive'. Maxine soon realised that the reason for higher
than average costs in SA was the pay and benefits offered to employees.

Maxine has a very different leadership style to Jo. She rarely comes out of her office and believes in giving
orders and setting targets. Maxine expects these targets to be met within departments. Maxine asked her
human resources (HR) director to set about building a flexible workforce. As employees left or retired, they
were replaced with new recruits on fixed-term, part-time and temporary contracts. Most new employees were
also given flexible contracts and seasonal workers were paid on a zero-hours basis. Only pilots and senior
managers are now on permanent contracts and Maxine feels that she has achieved her cost-cutting goal.

However, there have been disadvantages to Maxine's approach. The staff turnover rate has increased from 9 to
20 per cent per year, and many employees resent the high level of one-way communication that arrives via the
company's intranet system. Motivation levels among the flexible workforce are also falling, and some of these
employees resent others whose conditions of employment are more secure. The SA workplace representative
has been approached by many employees who are unhappy and he, in turn, has communicated this to the HR
director, as Maxine refused his request for a meeting. The level of employee absenteeism is also rising and
this can lead to flight delays while new crew members are called in. Also, there is some concern that there is
a labour market shortage of trained pilots and cabin crew, due to many more low-cost airlines starting up. The
recent recruitment campaign attracted very few high-quality applicants and Maxine's HR director has asked for
a meeting with her to discuss the problems. Maxine has agreed to a meeting in one week's time and has asked
for the key points of concern to be given to her in advance.

Discussion point

If you were Maxine's HR director, what questions would you submit for discussion at the meeting?

Exam-style questions: Case study

1 Analyse **two** pieces of evidence from the text that suggest that Jo Swift was a good leader. [8]

....

....

....

....

....

....

2 Analyse **two** different leaders and their roles in JS Airways. [8]

....

....

....

....

....

....

3 Evaluate whether Maxine's management style is the main reason for the problems with recruiting new employees at SA. [12]

....

....

....

....

....

....

....

4 Evaluate how Maxine might improve employee morale and continue to keep costs low at SA. [12]

....

....

....

....

....

....

....

....

5 Analyse **one** example of hard HRM and **one** example of soft HRM from the SA case study. [8]

....

....

....

....

....

....

....

6 Evaluate whether Maxine took the right decision to introduce flexible contracts in SA. [12]

....

....

....

....

....

....

....

7 Evaluate how the current HR problems at SA may be solved. Justify your recommendation. [12]

....

....

....

....

....

....

....

8 Marketing

8.1 Marketing analysis

KEY TERMS

Market analysis, price/income/promotional elasticity of demand, total revenue, product development, research and development (R&D), patent, total volume and value of sales, sales forecast, moving average, extrapolation, correlation, confidence level.

True/false questions

Decide whether each of the statements below is true or false. Circle the correct answer and explain your decision. Use an example from a business you have learnt about if appropriate.

1 Market analysis means looking at a company's past sales data. [3]

True/False

....

....

....

2 A product with an income elasticity of demand of –0.5 may be classified as an 'inferior' good. [3]

True/False

....

....

....

3 If a firm's promotional elasticity of demand is less than 1, this means increased spending on advertising will not increase sales. [3]

True/False

....

....

....

4 Spending on new product development will guarantee increased sales in the future. [3]

True/False

....

....

....

5 The likely correlation between ice cream sales and summer temperatures is negative. [3]

True/False

....

....

....

6 A company that is enjoying high sales in a growing market does not need to spend money on the research and development of new products. [3]

True/False

....

....

....

7 If a company is granted a patent on an innovative product design this means it will not face competition in the market. [3]

True/False

....

....

....

▶ 8.2 Marketing strategy

KEY TERMS

Marketing strategy/planning/objectives/budget, co-ordinated marketing strategy, information technology (IT) and artificial intelligence (AI) in marketing, international marketing, globalisation, World Trade Organization, protectionism, tariffs, quotas, pan-global strategy, localisation, limitations of marketing planning.

▶ True/false questions

Decide whether each of the statements below is true or false. Circle the correct answer and explain your decision. Use an example from a business you have learnt about if appropriate.

1 A marketing strategy is all about the 4Ps of the marketing mix. [3]

True/False

....

....

....

2 Marketing objectives must be closely related to corporate objectives. [3]

True/False

....

....

....

3 A country's government may impose a tariff to encourage more imports. [3]

True/False

....

....

....

4 Globalisation only leads to more marketing opportunities for big companies. [3]

True/False

....

....

5 Use of artificial intelligence (AI) in marketing has more benefits to companies than their customers. [3]

True/False

....

....

....

Research task

Do this individually or in small groups.

Create a presentation, with examples, about the difference between pan-global and localised international marketing strategies. Choose two multinational companies, one of which uses a pan-global strategy and one of which uses a more localised approach.

Answer the following question: Under what conditions is a pan-global strategy suitable, rather than catering for local differences between countries?

Case study: Marketing analysis and marketing strategy: Gio's Pizzas

Gio came from Italy, with his family, to a large city in India to start a company making and selling pizzas. He now owns three Gio's Pizzas (GP) restaurants in the city and intends to expand further into new locations, both in India and overseas. Gio's restaurants also offer a takeaway and delivery service, which is becoming increasingly popular as people prefer to eat at home, rather than going out. Incomes in GP's home city are rising and unemployment is falling.

Gio is sure that he knows the market for pizzas very well. He carries out regular market research and forecasts sales using past data, extrapolation and the moving average method. He also keeps a careful watch on eating trends. GP recently introduced a mobile phone app, which enables customers to book tables and order food online. Most of GP's marketing is also carried out through the website, but with the addition of leaflets with 'money off' vouchers regularly delivered throughout the city. Gio uses social media extensively in his marketing, and advises his customers about menu changes and special offers that suit their preferences.

Sales of pizzas have been rising for some years now, but Gio is worried that the product is going out of fashion. He has read articles in the press and blogs on social media which criticise pizzas as being 'unhealthy', and which blame the increasing obesity crisis on this and other fast food. Gio has also found that his sales forecasts have become less reliable and believes this is due to changing market trends.

Gio asked his daughter, Anna, to research alternative products that would use the same cooking and storage facilities. She has developed a new 'healthy living' menu, which includes pizzas prepared using thin, less fatty bases, with low-fat cheese, more vegetable toppings and vegan options. Additionally, there would also be a wide range of salads available.

Anna's research suggests the following elasticity data for the current and proposed new product ranges.

Table 8.1

Product range	Price elasticity of demand	Income elasticity of demand	Promotional elasticity of demand
Formula			
Current pizza range	–2.5	–0.7	0.6
Proposed new healthy living menu	–1.2	+1.5	1.8

Gio feels that this information, together with the fact that his sales forecasts suggest sales of the current product range will fall in the future, mean that launching the new 'healthy living' menu may be a good development for GP, but he knows the market is becoming very competitive. He has now asked Anna to carry out a SWOT analysis on GP and recommend a co-ordinated marketing strategy for the launch of the new menu.

Discussion point

Consider other examples of fast-food companies which have introduced healthy options in response to customer eating trends, such as veganism. Find examples of those which have been very successful and those which have been less successful. What are the factors that influence the success of a new product launch? Will a new product that works well in one country also do the same in another?

Exam-style questions: Case study

Before you start the questions, please fill in the elasticity formulae in the relevant boxes within the table above and review the meaning of these results.

1 Using the elasticity data in the table, analyse **two** differences between demand for the current pizza menu and the proposed new 'healthy living' menu. [8]

....

....

....

....

....

....

2 Evaluate whether Gio should change his methods of sales forecasting. Justify your conclusion. [12]

....

....

....

....

....

....

....

3 Using the elasticity data and other information from the case study, evaluate whether GP should introduce the new 'healthy living' menu. [12]

....

....

....

....

....

....

....

4 Evaluate a co-ordinated marketing strategy for the launch of the new 'healthy living' menu. Justify your recommendations. [12]

....

....

....

....

....

....

5 Evaluate whether a co-ordinated marketing strategy will guarantee the success of the new 'healthy living' menu. [12]

6 Evaluate the use of information technology (IT) and artificial intelligence (AI) for the future success of Gio's marketing strategy. [12]

7 Gio would like to expand GP into international markets. Evaluate whether a pan-global strategy would be the best approach to use. Justify your recommendation. [12]

9 Operations management

▶ **9.1** Location and scale

KEY TERMS

Location, relocation, offshoring, reshoring, foreign direct investment (FDI), scale of operations, output level, specialisation, economies/diseconomies of scale, internal and external economies/diseconomies of scale.

▶ True/false questions

Decide whether each of the statements below is true or false. Circle the correct answer and explain your decision. Use an example from a business you have learnt about if appropriate.

1 A car manufacturing company may locate a factory overseas to avoid trade barriers. [3]

   True/False

   ....

   ....

   ....

2 Reshoring is when a company moves production overseas, away from its home country. [3]

   True/False

   ....

   ....

   ....

3 Increasing globalisation is likely to lead to increasing foreign direct investment in developing countries. [3]

   True/False

   ....

   ....

   ....

4 Increasing the scale of operations will mean increased capacity. [3]

   True/False

   ....

   ....

   ....

5   A lack of local skilled labour may lead to internal economies of scale for a car manufacturer. [3]

True/False

....

....

....

Research task
● ●

Do this individually or in small groups.

Research a large, local manufacturing or warehousing organisation. Consider the likely reasons for the company choosing its current location. Think about cost, closeness to customers, any trade barriers and brand image. Write a report or presentation answering the following questions: Should the company relocate? If so, where to?

▶ 9.2 Quality management

> **KEY TERMS**
> Quality, fitness for use, quality targets/control/assurance, total quality management (TQM), internal customers, benchmarking.

▶ True/false questions
● ●

Decide whether each of the statements below is true or false. Circle the correct answer and explain your decision. Use an example from a business you have learnt about if appropriate.

1   A quality product is one that sells for a high price. [3]

True/False

....

....

....

2   Quality assurance means checking the product for defects at the end of the production process. [3]

True/False

....

....

....

3 The successful introduction of total quality management (TQM) means that quality inspectors will no longer be needed. [3]

True/False

....

....

....

4 An internal customer is someone who buys your product. [3]

True/False

....

....

5 Benchmarking means comparing aspects of a firm's operations with those of another firm in a different industry. [3]

True/False

....

....

....

Research task

Do this individually or in small groups.

Create a presentation, with examples, about the importance of quality in the fast-food industry. Include examples from local fast-food outlets that address the following questions:
» What is the meaning of quality in fast food?
» What quality targets might a new fast-food franchisee business owner set?
» How might TQM work within a fast-food outlet?

▶ **9.3** Operations strategy

KEY TERMS

Operations strategy, computer-aided design (CAD), computer-aided manufacturing (CAM), flexibility in operations, product/process innovation, enterprise resource planning (ERP), lean production, kaizen, quality circles, simultaneous engineering, cell production, just-in-time (JIT) production, waste management, operations planning, critical path analysis, network diagrams, free float, total float.

True/false questions

Decide whether each of the statements below is true or false. Circle the correct answer and explain your decision. Use an example from a business you have learnt about if appropriate.

1   The use of artificial intelligence (AI) means production by robots.   [3]

True/False

....

....

....

2   Increasing flexibility in operations should lead to lower unit costs.   [3]

True/False

....

....

....

3   Improving waste-management techniques will lead to great sustainability.   [3]

True/False

....

....

....

4   In a network diagram, critical tasks are those with the greatest float times.   [3]

True/False

....

....

....

5   Successful introduction of lean-production techniques always requires employee training.   [3]

True/False

....

....

....

> ## Research task
> ●
>
> *Do this individually or in small groups.*
>
> Does increased use of AI mean that, eventually, all human workers will be replaced by computers? Research different views on this and discuss it as a class.

Go Scooters

Go Scooters (GS) started as a toy manufacturer back in the 1950s, but is now a public limited company and a leading world producer of electric scooters. The scooters are assembled on a modern, automated production line in a factory located in Eastern Europe. GS also has factories located in several countries in Asia that produce the parts and accessories. Sales have increased fast over the last three years, as many countries now allow electric scooters as a means of transport in big cities. The main factory is now operating at 90 per cent capacity utilisation, with an output of 1.5 million scooters per year. There is an urgent need to increase the scale of operations in order to start production of a new, larger 'commuter scooter', with adult professional workers as its target market. The country in Eastern Europe where the GS factory is located is experiencing some political and economic instability.

The CEO of GS is Jodie. She is considering two possible options for expansion. One option is to double the size of the present factory by purchasing more land. The other is to build an assembly plant in one of the locations in Asia where some parts are already being manufactured. The operations director of GS has drawn up network diagrams for the two options. Jodie is concerned that some of the estimated timings for the factory in Asia may be optimistic. She has drawn up a table of advantages and disadvantages of the two options to present to her board of directors. At present, Jodie prefers the option of expanding the current factory, but the GS finance director is in favour of the factory in Asia, due to cost advantages.

Table 9.1

	Option 1 Expand current scooter assembly factory to produce commuter scooters	Option 2 Build a second factory to assemble commuter scooters in Asia
Initial cost comparison	$2.5 million	$2 million
Estimated project completion time from critical-path analysis/ network diagram	28 weeks	40 weeks
Advantages to GS	• Assembly of scooters remains on a single site • Existing factory management can be used • Existing technical equipment may be used, e.g. for safety testing • Current supply chain of parts can be used • Possibility of more specialisation in production	• Lower initial costs and ongoing wage costs will be lower • Easy access to fast-growing Asian markets for finished products • High-skilled labour available locally, including managers with experience of vehicle manufacture • Close to some parts manufacturers
Disadvantages to GS	• Shortage of skilled labour locally • Over-reliance on one location, in view of political and economic instability • Current management may be overburdened • Communication may become difficult as number of employees increases and two production lines are running	• Communication with main factory may be difficult, due to distance, language and cultural differences • Monitoring quality of new scooter model may be difficult • Design team for new scooters may not be willing to relocate

Jodie knows that quality and safety are vital both for the existing scooters and the new commuter scooters. They need to meet rigorous safety standards in every country in which they will be sold. Currently, GS operates a system of quality control, where scooters are checked and tested at the end of the manufacturing process, before they are sold. Currently, 10 per cent of this output is rejected as defective. Recently, production was delayed for a total of three days due to an error made in inventory ordering.

Jodie knows that increasing efficiency and cutting down waste in all areas of the business will be essential for future competitiveness. She would like to introduce lean-production techniques, including a total quality management (TQM) approach into both the existing and new production lines. However, the workers' representative has indicated that many current workers would resist this change. Jodie has asked for volunteers among the workforce to join a regular kaizen group, and some of the younger workers are keen to contribute ideas and take part in discussions.

Jodie has recently visited a large car factory, where the company uses enterprise resource planning (ERP) software to control resources and cut down on waste. The use of this system has enabled the car company to control inventory and ordering, as well as making more flexible use of the workforce. The factory manager explained that investment in employee training had played a vital role in the successful introduction of the system.

There are clearly going to be many changes within operations at GS. Jodie knows that these will be vital if GS is to maintain its competitiveness and increase its market share. Jodie has arranged a meeting for the whole company at which she will present plans for the new production line, as well as the move towards lean production in GS.

Discussion points

» How would you advise Jodie to introduce changes in operations strategy to the workforce?

» Why do you think existing employees at GS may resist the changes?

» How might these reasons for resistance be overcome?

Exam-style questions: Case study

1 Analyse **two** impacts of the current method of quality control used in GS.   [8]

....

....

....

....

....

....

2 Evaluate whether Jodie should introduce total quality management (TQM) at GS.   [12]

....

....

....

....

....

....

....

3 Using the table of advantages and disadvantages, and other information from the case study, evaluate whether GS should expand the current factory or build a new factory in Asia for production of the 'commuter scooter' model.   [12]

....

....

....

....

....

....

....

4   Analyse **two** benefits to GS of benchmarking its operations functions against the car manufacturer visited by Jodie.   [8]

....

....

....

....

....

....

5   Evaluate the best way for Jodie to introduce lean-production techniques to GS. Justify your recommendations.   [12]

....

....

....

....

....

....

6   Evaluate whether improving the effectiveness of operations will be the most important factor for the future success of GS.   [12]

....

....

....

....

....

....

10 Finance and accounting

 10.1 Financial statements

Table exercise

Review the important definitions and formulae, and fill in the table below.

Table 10.1

Term	Definition	Formula
Statement of profit or loss (income statement)		
Profit		
Loss		
Gross profit		
Profit from operations (operating profit)		
Profit for the year		
Dividends (distributed profit)		
Retained earnings (retained profit)		
Statement of financial position		
Assets		
Revenue		
Non-current assets		
Current assets		

Term	Definition	Formula
Capital		
Liabilities		
Non-current liabilities		
Current liabilities		
Net current assets		
Cost of sales		
Expenses		
Net assets		
Equity		
Liquidity		
Reserves		
Depreciation		
Straight-line method of depreciation		
Inventory		
Net realisable value method		
Taxation		

XY Traders

The following tables and questions are based on XY Traders, a successful food-processing and packaging company located in a small country in Africa. Their main products are sugar, cocoa powder, coffee and dried fruits.

XY Traders is owned and run by the Mulenga family, who are keen to expand and invite new investors to buy shares.

Table 10.2 Estimated statement of profit or loss (income statement) for XY Traders as at 31 December 2022

	$'000 (estimated)	$'000 (amended)
Revenue (220000 units @ $5)	1 100	
Cost of sales (@ $2 per unit)	440	
Gross profit	660	
Overhead expenses	200	
Operating profit	460	
Finance costs (interest)	30	
Profit before tax	430	
Corporation tax @ 20%	86	
Profit for the year	344	
Dividends paid	150	
Retained earnings	194	

1 Assume the following changes and amend the statement of profit or loss figures in the right-hand column of Table 10.2 above. [10]
   » Each unit was sold for $4.50.
   » Cost of sales for each unit rose to $2.10.
   » Overheads fell by 5 per cent.
   » Finance costs fell by 30 per cent.
   » Corporation tax per cent and dividends remain the same.

Table 10.3 Estimated statement of financial position for XY Traders as at 31 December 2022

ASSETS	$'000 (estimated)	$'000	$'000 (amended)	$'000
Non-current assets				
Property	3000			
Equipment	400			
	3400			
Current assets				
Inventories	200			
Accounts receivable	55			
Cash	60			
	315			
TOTAL ASSETS		3715		
EQUITY and LIABILITIES				
Current liabilities				
Accounts payable	300			
Overdraft	60			
	360			
Non-current liabilities				

ASSETS	$'000 (estimated)	$'000	$'000 (amended)	$'000
Long-term loans	700			
	700			
TOTAL LIABILITIES	1060			
Shareholders' equity				
Share capital	2000			
Retained earnings	655			
	2655			
TOTAL EQUITY and LIABILITIES		3715		

Note on calculation of capital employed: *There are different methods of calculating capital employed, but for the purposes of this course, capital employed = total equity + non-current liabilities*

2 Assume the following changes and amend the statement of financial position figures in the right-hand columns of Table 10.3 above. [10]
 » The property assets have increased in value by buying a new building for $400 000, financed by an increase in share capital and a further long-term loan (50 per cent of the cost from each).
 » Some inventories have remained unsold and have had to be disposed of, so value of inventories has decreased by 15 per cent.
 » The company's overdraft has increased by 20 per cent.
 » The retained earnings figure, part of shareholders' equity, has to be adjusted to make sure the statement of financial position still balances.

3 XY Traders are planning to purchase new machinery for $120 000. It is expected to last for five years and the residual value at the end of this time will be $10 000.

 a Calculate the annual depreciation charge for the machinery, using the straight-line method. [3]

 ....

 ....

 ....

 b Explain how this annual depreciation would be accounted for in the statement of profit or loss and the statement of financial position. [3]

 ....

 ....

 ....

4 XY Traders has some inventories that it bought two years ago for $30 000. It will no longer be possible to sell these at the usual price. Another supplier has offered to buy these for $20 000, but also wants XY to deliver, which will cost $2000. Using the concept of net realisable value, calculate and explain how these inventories must be valued on the statement of financial position. [4]

 ....

 ....

 ....

 ....

▶ **10.2** Analysis of published accounts

Table exercise

Review the important definitions and formulae, and fill in the table below.

Table 10.4

Ratio	Formula and units (Remember that units vary. Some are % but others are number of times, decimals, days, etc.)	What the ratio tells us about a business (e.g. likely recommended value)
Liquidity ratios		
Current ratio		
Acid test ratio		
Profitability ratios		
Gross profit margin		
Profit margin		
Capital employed		
Return on capital employed		
Financial efficiency ratios		
Inventory turnover ratio		
Trade payables turnover (days)		
Trade receivables turnover (days)		
Gearing		
Gearing ratio		
Investment ratios		
Dividend per share		
Dividend yield		
Dividend cover ratio		
Price/earnings ratio		
Window dressing (explanation of this term)		

Exam-style questions

Refer back to the XY Traders case study in Chapter 10.1. Use the estimated figures in the statement of profit or loss and statement of financial position to answer the following questions.

1 Using Table 10.2 and Table 10.3, calculate the following profit margins for XY Traders:

   a Gross profit margin [2]

   ....

   ....

   b Operating profit margin [2]

   ....

   ....

   c Return on capital employed (ROCE) [2]

....

....

2 Analyse **two** ways in which XY Traders could improve the company's profitability. [8]

....

....

....

....

....

....

3 Using Table 10.3, calculate the following liquidity ratios for XY Traders:

   a Current ratio [2]

....

....

   b Acid test ratio [2]

....

....

4 Analyse **two** ways in which XY Traders could improve the company's liquidity. [8]

....

....

....

....

....

....

5 Using Table 10.2 and Table 10.3, calculate the inventory turnover ratio for XY Traders. (Assume that the inventory figure in Table 10.3 is also the average inventory figure.) [2]

....

....

6 Using Table 10.3 and assuming that the new building is purchased for $400 000, is 50 per cent financed by a long-term loan and 50 per cent by an increase in share capital, calculate the change in the gearing ratio for XY Traders.

a Gearing before new investment [2]

....

....

b Gearing after new investment [2]

....

....

7 The current share price of XY Traders is $4 and the number of shares issued is 40 000. Using other information from Table 10.2, calculate the following:

a The dividend per share [2]

....

....

b XY's dividend cover ratio [2]

....

....

c XY's price/earnings ratio [2]

....

....

8 Using your ratio calculations and other information, would you recommend a new investor to buy shares in XY Traders? [12]

....

....

....

....

....

....

....

....

10.3 Investment appraisal

KEY TERMS

Investment appraisal, net cash flow, systemic/specific risks, payback method, accounting rate of return method, discount factors, discounted cash flow, net present value, qualitative factors (corporate image/objectives, environmental/ethical issues, industrial relations).

Table exercise

Complete the table below about the different investment appraisal methods.

Table 10.5

Investment appraisal method	Description/what it shows	How to calculate, including any relevant formula
Payback		
Accounting rate of return (ARR)		
Net present value (NPV)		

Exam-style questions

Refer back to the XY Traders case study in Chapter 10.1 to answer these questions.

XY Traders are considering two factory expansion projects. They can only choose one of these. The project that is chosen will be financed by bank borrowing at 8 per cent interest.

Option 1 is an expansion into a neighbouring country, and option 2 is modernisation and automation of an existing factory. Option 1 will cost $1.5 million and option 2 will cost $2 million.

Table 10.6 Estimated net cash-flow figures for expansion projects (figures in brackets are negative)

(All figures in $'000)			
	Option 1	Option 2	Discount factor
Year	Expansion into a neighbouring country	Existing factory automation	@ 10%
0	(1 500)	(2 000)	1
1	400	300	0.91
2	500	400	0.83
3	500	500	0.75
4	500	700	0.68
5	600	800	0.62

1 Calculate the payback period, accounting rate of return (ARR) and net present value (NPV) of the two options and two possible qualitative factors for each. Collate your information in Table 10.7 below. [12]

Table 10.7

	Option 1	Option 2
Payback period		
Accounting rate of return (ARR)		
Net present value (NPV)		
Possible qualitative factors for consideration	1 2	1 2

2 Use your results to question 1, and other information on qualitative factors, to evaluate which will be the best option for XY Traders to choose. Justify your recommendation. [12]

....

....

....

....

....

....

....

....

10.4 Finance and accounting strategy

> **KEY TERMS**
>
> Strategic decision-making, chief financial officer, liquidity, annual report, key performance indicators, ratio benchmarking, time series financial data, capital structure, debt, equity, dividend strategy, overtrading, window dressing, limitations of the use of accounting data and ratios.

Exam-style questions

Before answering these questions, please review the financial and other information in the previous three sections about XY Traders.

1 Analyse **two** financial ratios that you have calculated that will be important to XY Traders' ability to raise finance. [8]

....

....

....

....

....

....

2 Identify **four** stakeholder groups who may be interested in XY Traders' annual report. Complete the table below with the stakeholder groups and how they might use the information. [8]

Table 10.8

Stakeholder group	Interest and analysis of how the annual report information might be used

3 Evaluate the importance of interfirm comparison and benchmarking of financial ratios to XY Traders. [12]

....

....

....

....

....

....

....

4 Evaluate the impact of business growth through option 1 or option 2 on the financial ratios of
XY Traders. [12]

....

....

....

....

....

....

....

5 'Shareholder ratios are the most important influence on potential investors when they are considering
buying shares in a business such as XY Traders.' Evaluate this statement. [12]

....

....

....

....

....

....

....

Practise and apply what you have studied and develop independent learning skills by answering a range of questions and activities that are clearly linked to the content of the Student's Book.

» Build confidence with extra practice to ensure that a topic is thoroughly understood before moving on.

» Explore and analyse international businesses through data response questions based on real case studies.

» Keep track of your work with ready-to-go write-in exercises.

» Answers can be found at **hoddereducation.com/cambridgeextras**.

Cambridge International AS & A Level

Business

Second edition

Malcolm Surridge
Andrew Gillespie

Use with *Cambridge International AS & A Level Business Student's Book Second Edition*
9781398308114

For over 25 years we have been trusted by Cambridge schools around the world to provide quality support for teaching and learning. For this reason we have been selected by Cambridge Assessment International Education as an official publisher of endorsed material for their syllabuses.

This resource is endorsed by Cambridge Assessment International Education

✓ Provides learner support for the Cambridge International AS & A Level Business syllabus (9609) for examination from 2023

✓ Has passed Cambridge International's rigorous quality-assurance process

✓ Developed by subject experts

✓ For Cambridge schools worldwide

HODDER EDUCATION
e: education@hachette.co.uk
w: hoddereducation.com

ISBN 978-1-398-30815-2

MIX
Paper from responsible sources
FSC™ C104740